Digitalizing Nature-Based Solutions: Harnessing Technology for Climate Resilience and Sustainable Ecosystems

Copyright

Author:

Robert C. Brears

Publisher:

Global Climate Solutions

The views expressed in this publication are those of the author. The publisher, while a separate entity, shares the same views and supports the perspectives presented.

Disclaimer:

This publication is intended for informational purposes only. While every effort has been made to ensure accuracy, the author and publisher accept no responsibility for any errors or omissions, or for any consequences arising from the use of the material contained herein. Readers are advised to seek appropriate professional guidance where necessary.

ISBNs:

eBook: 978-1-991369-31-4

Paperback: 978-1-991369-32-1

First Edition

Table of Contents

Conclusion

Preface

In recent years, the call for nature-based solutions (NBS) has gained momentum, driven by the urgency to address global climate change, biodiversity loss, and urban sustainability. While the principles of working with nature are not new, the scale and complexity of today's environmental challenges demand innovative tools and approaches to enhance the design, implementation, and scalability of these solutions. This is where digital technologies enter the picture—not as a replacement for nature, but as vital enablers that amplify its potential.

This book, *Digitalizing Nature-Based Solutions: Harnessing Technology for Climate Resilience and Sustainable Ecosystems*, explores the dynamic intersection of technology and ecology. As someone who has worked extensively in the fields of climate resilience, water governance, and sustainability strategy, I have seen first-hand how digital tools are transforming the way we understand and manage natural systems. From Geographic Information Systems (GIS) that map vulnerable ecosystems to the Internet of Things (IoT) sensors that monitor environmental health in real time, these technologies are revolutionizing how we design, monitor, and scale up NBS.

The purpose of this book is not to celebrate technology for its own sake but to examine critically and constructively how digital innovation can support and enhance nature-based approaches. It offers readers a comprehensive and structured overview of key digital technologies—from Artificial Intelligence (AI) and blockchain to digital twin technology—and their relevance to nature-based interventions across urban, rural, and coastal contexts. It also considers the governance, equity, and ethical dimensions of digitalizing NBS, recognizing that these solutions must be inclusive, adaptive, and rooted in ecological integrity.

Each chapter is designed to serve both as a standalone insight and as part of a larger narrative that connects emerging technologies with ecological thinking. The goal is to provide practitioners, researchers, and policymakers with the conceptual tools and practical frameworks needed to leverage digital innovation while maintaining the ecological and community-based foundations of NBS.

As digitalization accelerates, it is my hope that this book serves as a timely and valuable resource for those working at the forefront of climate adaptation and environmental sustainability. By bridging the digital and the natural, we can develop smarter, more resilient ecosystems that not only withstand the pressures of a changing world but also thrive within it.

— *Robert C. Brears*

Introduction: Unlocking the Potential of Digital Innovation in Nature-Based Solutions

NBS have gained significant attention as a means to address environmental challenges while promoting sustainability. By leveraging natural processes, NBS provide cost-effective and adaptable approaches to issues such as climate resilience, biodiversity conservation, and water resource management. However, their implementation and scalability often face obstacles, including resource constraints, limited monitoring capabilities, and the complexities of managing ecosystems in a changing climate.

The integration of digital technologies into NBS offers new opportunities to overcome these challenges. Tools such as GIS, AI, and the IoT enable improved planning, monitoring, and management of these solutions. These technologies can enhance the precision, efficiency, and impact of NBS, making them more accessible and effective in diverse contexts.

This book examines how digital innovation is transforming NBS. It explores the role of technology in optimizing design and implementation, facilitating data-driven decision-making, and engaging stakeholders. The chapters ahead will provide a comprehensive overview of how specific digital tools contribute to the development of NBS, from urban green infrastructure to watershed restoration.

By maintaining a neutral and analytical tone, this book aims to offer insights into the evolving relationship between technology and NBS. It is not a call for the wholesale replacement of traditional practices but rather an exploration of how digitalization can complement and enhance nature-based approaches. Through this lens, the book seeks to provide a deeper understanding of the opportunities and challenges associated with digitalizing NBS.

Definition of Nature-Based Solutions

NBS are actions that leverage natural processes and ecosystems to address societal challenges. According to the International Union for Conservation of Nature (IUCN), NBS are defined as "actions to protect, sustainably manage, and restore natural or modified ecosystems that address societal challenges effectively and adaptively, simultaneously providing human well-being and biodiversity benefits."

These solutions involve working with nature rather than against it, using approaches such as reforestation, wetland restoration, urban green spaces, and sustainable agricultural practices. By enhancing the health and functionality of ecosystems, NBS provide multiple co-benefits, including climate change mitigation and adaptation, improved biodiversity, and enhanced human health and well-being.

Importance of NBS in Addressing Climate Change

NBS are increasingly recognized as essential tools in tackling the climate crisis. They contribute to both climate change mitigation and adaptation:

1. **Mitigation**:

• NBS such as afforestation, mangrove restoration, and peatland conservation sequester carbon dioxide from the atmosphere, helping to reduce greenhouse gas concentrations.

• Healthy ecosystems act as carbon sinks, with forests alone storing approximately 80% of terrestrial above-ground carbon.

2. **Adaptation**:

• NBS strengthen the resilience of communities and ecosystems to climate impacts. For instance, wetlands and mangroves reduce the risk of flooding and storm surges, while urban green spaces help lower urban heat island effects.

• They promote water retention in landscapes, ensuring resources during droughts and mitigating the impacts of extreme weather events.

NBS and Sustainability Challenges

In addition to climate change, NBS address broader sustainability challenges:

1. Biodiversity Conservation:

• By protecting and restoring ecosystems, NBS help halt biodiversity loss and enhance habitats for wildlife.

2. Water Security:

• NBS, such as watershed management and natural filtration systems, improve water quality and availability while reducing pollution and erosion.

3. Urban Sustainability:

• Integrating NBS into urban planning, such as green roofs and permeable pavements, promotes sustainable cities by improving air quality, reducing energy use, and enhancing urban livability.

4. Human Well-being:

• NBS support physical and mental health through access to green spaces and cleaner environments.

By aligning with the goals of the Paris Agreement and the United Nations Sustainable Development Goals (SDGs), NBS provide a pathway for achieving climate resilience and sustainable development. They emphasize the interconnection between human well-being, biodiversity, and ecological health, highlighting their importance as multifaceted solutions in addressing the environmental challenges of the 21st century.

The Emerging Role of Digital Technologies in Nature-Based Solutions

Digital technologies are increasingly being recognized as transformative tools for enhancing the implementation, monitoring, and scalability of NBS. These technologies offer innovative ways to address the complexity of managing ecosystems, optimize resource use, and improve the effectiveness of NBS in tackling environmental challenges.

1. Enhancing Implementation

Digital technologies provide precision and efficiency in the design and implementation of NBS:

• **Data-Driven Planning**: GIS and remote sensing enable detailed mapping and spatial analysis of ecosystems, helping to identify optimal sites for interventions such as reforestation or wetland restoration.

• **Simulation and Modeling**: Digital twin technologies simulate ecosystem interactions, allowing stakeholders to test various NBS designs before physical implementation, thereby reducing risks and costs.

• **Automation and AI**: AI can process vast datasets to predict ecosystem responses, aiding in the design of solutions tailored to specific environmental and social contexts.

2. Improving Monitoring and Management

Once implemented, NBS require continuous monitoring to ensure their effectiveness and adapt to changing conditions. Digital technologies facilitate this through:

• **Real-Time Monitoring**: IoT sensors collect data on parameters such as water quality, soil health, and air pollution, providing real-time insights into ecosystem conditions.

• **Remote Monitoring**: Satellite imagery and drones allow for the regular observation of large-scale NBS projects, even in remote or inaccessible areas, reducing the need for on-site inspections.

• **Predictive Analytics**: Machine learning models analyze data trends to predict ecosystem responses to environmental changes, enabling proactive management and adaptation of NBS.

3. Supporting Scalability

Scaling NBS to meet global sustainability goals requires overcoming barriers such as resource limitations and coordination challenges. Digital technologies address these barriers by:

• **Collaboration Platforms**: Digital platforms facilitate communication and collaboration among stakeholders, including governments, NGOs, and local communities, ensuring coordinated action in large-scale projects.

• **Blockchain for Accountability**: Blockchain technology enhances transparency in NBS funding and implementation, building trust among stakeholders and ensuring that resources are allocated efficiently.

• **Cloud Computing and Big Data**: The ability to store and process large datasets in the cloud supports the analysis and replication of successful NBS models across different regions.

Unlocking the Full Potential of NBS

The integration of digital technologies with NBS has the potential to transform how ecosystems are managed and utilized for addressing climate change and sustainability challenges. By enabling precise design, efficient monitoring, and effective scaling, these technologies ensure that NBS achieve maximum impact while reducing costs and resource use.

However, the adoption of digital tools also raises challenges, such as ensuring equitable access to technology, addressing data privacy concerns, and balancing technological innovation with ecological sensitivity. As these challenges are addressed, digital technologies will play an increasingly vital role in enhancing the effectiveness and scalability of NBS, making them indispensable in the global effort toward sustainability and resilience.

Chapter 1: Understanding the Synergy Between Technology and Nature-Based Solutions

NBS have gained recognition for their ability to address environmental challenges by leveraging natural systems. However, their complexity, dynamic nature, and scalability often require innovative approaches to ensure effective implementation. Digital technologies, from data analysis tools to advanced monitoring systems, offer unprecedented opportunities to enhance the planning, execution, and management of NBS.

This chapter explores the foundational concepts behind the integration of technology with NBS. It examines the principles of NBS and their multifaceted benefits, while highlighting the growing role of digital innovation in overcoming traditional limitations. By understanding the synergy between these two domains, readers will gain insights into how technological advancements can complement and amplify the impact of nature-based approaches, creating more efficient and adaptable solutions for sustainability.

Overview of NBS Principles and Their Application in Urban, Rural, and Marine Environments

NBS are increasingly recognized as effective approaches to address a variety of environmental and societal challenges. By leveraging natural processes and ecosystems, NBS offer sustainable, adaptable, and often cost-effective solutions to enhance resilience, improve biodiversity, and support human well-being. To understand the potential of NBS, it is essential to examine the guiding principles that underpin their design and implementation, as well as their practical applications across urban, rural, and marine environments.

Principles of Nature-Based Solutions

NBS are founded on a set of principles that ensure their effectiveness, sustainability, and alignment with ecological and social goals. These principles include:

1. Ecosystem-Based Approach

NBS work with nature rather than against it, leveraging the inherent functions of ecosystems to deliver benefits. For example, restoring wetlands not only reduces flooding but also provides habitats for wildlife and improves water quality.

2. Multifunctionality

A key feature of NBS is their ability to deliver multiple benefits simultaneously. For instance, urban green spaces can reduce heat islands, improve air quality, and promote mental and physical health.

3. Sustainability

NBS prioritize long-term ecological health and societal benefits. This involves using renewable resources, minimizing environmental impacts, and ensuring that solutions remain effective under changing conditions.

4. Adaptive Management

NBS are designed to evolve in response to environmental and societal changes. This requires continuous monitoring and flexibility to adjust strategies as needed.

5. Inclusivity and Equity

Effective NBS incorporate the needs and perspectives of diverse stakeholders, including local communities, governments, and private entities. This ensures that solutions are socially equitable and culturally appropriate.

6. Cost-Effectiveness

While NBS often require initial investments, they can be more cost-effective than engineered solutions in the long term. For example, mangrove restoration can provide natural flood protection without the need for costly infrastructure.

Applications of NBS in Urban, Rural, and Marine Environments

The flexibility and adaptability of NBS allow them to be applied in various contexts, each with its unique challenges and opportunities. Below, we explore their applications in urban, rural, and marine environments.

1. Urban Environments

Urban areas face significant challenges, including air pollution, urban heat islands, stormwater management, and limited green spaces. NBS offer innovative solutions to these issues:

• **Green Infrastructure:**

Green roofs, vertical gardens, and urban forests enhance urban resilience by reducing heat, improving air quality, and promoting biodiversity. For example, urban tree planting helps sequester carbon, reduce temperatures, and provide aesthetic and recreational value.

• **Stormwater Management:**

Permeable pavements, rain gardens, and constructed wetlands manage stormwater effectively by mimicking natural hydrological processes. These solutions reduce flooding risks and improve water quality by filtering pollutants.

• **Biodiversity and Connectivity:**

Urban green corridors and parks create habitats for wildlife and enhance connectivity between fragmented ecosystems. This contributes to greater biodiversity within cities and fosters community engagement with nature.

• **Improved Livability:**

NBS in urban areas contribute to human well-being by reducing noise, providing recreational spaces, and improving mental health through access to natural environments.

2. Rural Environments

In rural settings, NBS address issues such as land degradation, water scarcity, and biodiversity loss. These solutions often focus on enhancing the productivity and sustainability of agricultural landscapes and restoring degraded ecosystems:

• **Sustainable Agriculture:**

Agroforestry practices, such as integrating trees with crops or livestock, improve soil health, reduce erosion, and enhance biodiversity. Similarly, crop rotation and cover cropping improve agricultural resilience to climate change.

• **Watershed Management:**

Reforestation and riparian buffer zones protect water resources by preventing soil erosion, filtering pollutants, and stabilizing streambanks. These measures ensure clean and reliable water supplies for communities and ecosystems.

• Habitat Restoration:

Projects to restore grasslands, peatlands, and forests enhance carbon sequestration, support biodiversity, and provide ecosystem services like water regulation and erosion control.

• Disaster Risk Reduction:

Planting windbreaks and constructing natural floodplains reduce the impact of extreme weather events, such as storms and floods, protecting both ecosystems and communities.

3. Marine and Coastal Environments

Marine and coastal ecosystems are vital for global biodiversity, food security, and climate regulation. However, these areas are increasingly under threat from human activity and climate change. NBS provide effective strategies to restore and protect these critical ecosystems:

• Mangrove Restoration:

Mangroves protect coastlines from erosion, storm surges, and tsunamis while also acting as carbon sinks. Restoring mangroves can stabilize coastal areas and support marine biodiversity.

• Seagrass and Coral Reef Restoration:

Seagrass beds sequester significant amounts of carbon and improve water quality, while coral reefs provide habitats for marine species and buffer coastlines from waves. Restoration efforts in these ecosystems enhance their ecological and economic benefits.

• **Living Shorelines:**

Unlike traditional seawalls, living shorelines use natural materials such as plants and oyster reefs to protect against coastal erosion. These solutions also create habitats for marine life and enhance water quality.

• **Sustainable Fisheries:**

Incorporating marine protected areas and ecosystem-based approaches to fisheries management ensures long-term sustainability. These measures help replenish fish stocks, support livelihoods, and maintain ecological balance.

Exploration of Digitalization as a Catalyst for Optimizing NBS Outcomes

NBS have demonstrated their potential to address pressing environmental challenges, such as climate change, biodiversity loss, and resource scarcity. However, the successful implementation and scalability of NBS often face challenges, including limited resources, complex ecosystem dynamics, and the need for ongoing monitoring and adaptation. Digitalization offers transformative tools and techniques to overcome these barriers, acting as a catalyst for optimizing the outcomes of NBS. By integrating digital technologies such as GIS, AI, and IoT devices, NBS can achieve greater precision, efficiency, and scalability.

1. Enhancing Design and Planning

Digitalization allows for more sophisticated planning and design of NBS, ensuring that interventions are both ecologically effective and economically viable.

• **Geographic Information Systems and Spatial Analysis:**

GIS enables detailed mapping of ecosystems, identifying areas best suited for NBS interventions. For example, in urban planning, GIS can pinpoint locations for green infrastructure, such as parks or wetlands, based on factors like flood risk, population density, and biodiversity hotspots.

• **Predictive Modeling:**

Tools like predictive models and simulations help forecast the potential outcomes of different NBS designs under varying environmental conditions. For instance, digital twin technology can simulate the impact of reforestation on carbon sequestration or predict how restored wetlands will influence water quality during extreme weather events.

• **Data-Driven Decision Making:**

Digital platforms collect and analyze vast amounts of environmental data, providing evidence-based recommendations for NBS planning. These platforms allow policymakers and stakeholders to make informed decisions by visualizing the trade-offs and benefits of various solutions.

2. Real-Time Monitoring and Management

Once implemented, NBS require ongoing monitoring and adaptive management to ensure their success over time. Digital tools significantly enhance these processes:

• **Internet of Things Devices:**

IoT sensors provide real-time data on environmental conditions, such as soil moisture, air quality, and water levels. For example, sensors installed in a wetland can continuously monitor water flow and nutrient levels, ensuring that the ecosystem functions as intended.

• **Remote Sensing and Drones:**

Satellite imagery and drones enable the regular monitoring of NBS across large or remote areas. These technologies reduce the need for frequent on-site visits, saving time and resources. For instance, drones can track the growth of mangroves or monitor vegetation cover in reforested areas.

• **Artificial Intelligence for Predictive Maintenance:**

AI algorithms analyze real-time data to identify patterns and predict potential issues. For example, an AI system might detect early signs of erosion in a green roof or identify areas of a reforested landscape that are not thriving. By addressing these issues proactively, managers can optimize the performance of NBS.

3. Improving Stakeholder Collaboration

NBS often involve multiple stakeholders, including governments, NGOs, businesses, and local communities. Digital platforms facilitate collaboration and engagement, ensuring that all voices are heard and resources are used efficiently:

• **Digital Platforms for Stakeholder Coordination:**

Platforms such as cloud-based dashboards allow stakeholders to share data, track progress, and make collaborative decisions. These tools enhance transparency and accountability, fostering trust among participants.

• **Community Engagement Tools:**

Apps and virtual reality (VR) tools can engage communities by providing interactive experiences that explain the purpose and benefits of NBS. For example, a VR simulation might demonstrate how a restored mangrove forest protects a coastal village from storm surges.

• Crowdsourcing and Citizen Science:

Digital tools enable the collection of data from local communities, such as reports on wildlife sightings or environmental changes. This crowdsourced data enriches decision-making processes and strengthens the connection between communities and their natural environment.

4. Scaling and Replicating Success

Scaling up NBS to address global challenges requires efficient replication of successful models. Digitalization plays a key role in enabling scalability:

• Big Data Analytics:

By analyzing large datasets from multiple NBS projects, digital tools identify patterns and best practices that can be applied in new contexts. For example, data from successful urban green infrastructure projects can inform similar efforts in other cities.

• Blockchain for Transparency and Funding:

Blockchain technology ensures transparent tracking of financial resources and project outcomes. This builds trust among investors and donors, facilitating the funding of larger and more ambitious NBS projects.

• Digital Twin Technology for Replication:

Digital twins create virtual models of successful NBS projects, allowing stakeholders to replicate these interventions in new locations with similar conditions. This reduces the time and resources needed for trial-and-error approaches.

5. Addressing Challenges and Barriers

While digitalization offers numerous advantages, it also presents challenges that must be addressed to fully realize its potential in optimizing NBS outcomes:

• Digital Divide:

Unequal access to technology can exclude certain communities from benefiting from digitalized NBS. Ensuring digital inclusivity is critical to the equitable implementation of these solutions.

• Data Privacy and Security:

Collecting and sharing large amounts of environmental and personal data require robust systems to protect privacy and prevent misuse.

• Balancing Technology with Ecological Sensitivity:

Over-reliance on technology risks overshadowing the ecological and community-driven aspects of NBS. Striking the right balance between technological and natural solutions is essential for sustainable outcomes.

Theoretical Framework for Integrating Technology with Natural Systems

The integration of technology with natural systems represents a transformative approach to addressing environmental and societal challenges. By combining the strengths of digital innovation with the inherent resilience and multifunctionality of ecosystems, this framework provides a foundation for designing and implementing

NBS that are efficient, adaptive, and scalable. Developing a theoretical framework for this integration involves understanding the interplay between ecological principles, technological capabilities, and the socioeconomic contexts in which NBS operate.

1. Core Principles of Integration

The framework for integrating technology with natural systems is built on the following principles:

a. Complementarity

Technology should complement natural processes rather than replace or disrupt them. For example, IoT sensors can monitor water levels in wetlands without interfering with their ecological functions.

b. Systems Thinking

Natural systems are complex and interconnected. A systems approach considers the dynamic relationships between various components of an ecosystem, ensuring that technological interventions align with and enhance these interactions.

c. Adaptability

Both natural systems and technologies are subject to change. The framework emphasizes adaptive management, allowing NBS to evolve in response to environmental conditions and technological advancements.

d. Sustainability

Technological solutions must align with the principles of sustainability, ensuring minimal environmental impact and long-term viability.

e. Inclusivity

The integration process should involve diverse stakeholders, including local communities, governments, and private sectors, ensuring that the solutions are equitable and culturally appropriate.

2. Key Components of the Framework

The theoretical framework comprises three key components: ecological systems, digital technologies, and the interface between them.

a. Ecological Systems

Natural systems form the foundation of NBS and are characterized by their ability to provide ecosystem services such as carbon sequestration, water purification, and biodiversity conservation. The framework identifies the following ecological considerations:

• **Ecosystem Dynamics:** Understanding the structure, function, and processes of ecosystems is essential for designing effective interventions.

• **Service Provisioning:** Identifying the specific ecosystem services to be enhanced or restored guides the selection of appropriate technologies.

• **Thresholds and Resilience:** Recognizing the limits of ecosystem capacity ensures that interventions do not push natural systems beyond their thresholds.

b. Digital Technologies

The framework emphasizes the role of digital tools in enhancing the design, implementation, and management of NBS. Key technological components include:

• **Data Collection and Analysis:** IoT sensors, drones, and remote sensing technologies provide real-time data on ecosystem health and function.

• **Modeling and Simulation:** AI and machine learning enable the prediction of ecosystem responses to various interventions, supporting data-driven decision-making.

• **Collaboration and Transparency:** Blockchain and digital platforms enhance stakeholder coordination, trust, and accountability in NBS projects.

c. Interface Between Technology and Nature

The interface is where technology and natural systems interact to achieve desired outcomes. This requires:

• **Design for Integration:** Technologies must be designed to operate seamlessly within ecosystems, minimizing disturbance and maximizing benefits.

• **Feedback Mechanisms:** Continuous data collection and analysis provide feedback loops for adaptive management, ensuring that interventions remain effective over time.

• **Scalability:** The framework considers how technologies can be scaled to apply successful NBS models across different contexts and geographies.

3. Steps for Implementing the Framework

To operationalize the theoretical framework, the following steps are proposed:

a. Assessment and Baseline Analysis

• Conduct a comprehensive assessment of the ecosystem, identifying its current state, challenges, and opportunities.

• Establish baseline conditions for monitoring the impact of interventions.

b. Technology Selection and Customization

• Choose technologies that align with the ecological, social, and economic context of the NBS project.

• Customize tools to ensure they address specific ecosystem needs and stakeholder priorities.

c. Co-Design with Stakeholders

• Engage stakeholders in the design process to ensure solutions are inclusive and culturally appropriate.

• Use participatory methods, such as workshops and focus groups, to integrate local knowledge and preferences.

d. Pilot Testing and Iteration

• Implement pilot projects to test the integration of technology with natural systems.

• Use feedback from pilots to refine both technological tools and ecological interventions.

e. Implementation and Monitoring

• Scale up successful pilot projects, ensuring the integration of continuous monitoring systems.

• Use data-driven insights to adapt and improve interventions over time.

f. Evaluation and Knowledge Sharing

• Conduct evaluations to measure the effectiveness of the integrated approach.

• Share findings through digital platforms and networks to support broader adoption and learning.

4. Challenges and Considerations

Integrating technology with natural systems is not without challenges. The framework acknowledges and seeks to address the following issues:

• **Technological Over-Reliance:** Overuse of technology risks overshadowing the ecological foundations of NBS. Balance is crucial.

• **Equity in Access:** Ensuring that all stakeholders, particularly marginalized communities, have access to digital tools and benefits.

• **Data Privacy and Security:** Safeguarding sensitive data collected from ecosystems and communities.

• **Cost and Resource Constraints:** Managing the costs associated with advanced technologies to ensure affordability and scalability.

5. Potential Applications of the Framework

The theoretical framework is versatile and can be applied across a range of NBS projects:

• **Urban Green Infrastructure:** Integrating IoT sensors and GIS mapping to design and monitor urban parks, green roofs, and stormwater systems.

• **Coastal Restoration:** Using drones and remote sensing to track mangrove growth and assess coastal protection effectiveness.

• **Agricultural Resilience:** Employing AI to optimize agroforestry practices and predict crop responses to changing climates.

Chapter 2: Geographic Information Systems and Remote Sensing in Nature-Based Solutions

GIS and remote sensing technologies have become essential tools in planning, implementing, and monitoring NBS. These technologies enable a deeper understanding of ecosystems by providing accurate spatial data, identifying critical areas for intervention, and monitoring changes over time. From mapping urban green infrastructure to tracking deforestation or wetland restoration, GIS and remote sensing provide the precision and insights necessary for effective decision-making.

This chapter explores the applications of GIS and remote sensing in NBS, focusing on their role in mapping, planning, and monitoring projects in diverse contexts, including urban, rural, and marine environments. It also examines the opportunities and challenges associated with scaling these technologies for broader adoption, setting the stage for their integration with other digital tools in advancing sustainable solutions.

The Role of GIS and Remote Sensing in Mapping, Planning, and Monitoring NBS Projects

GIS and remote sensing technologies have emerged as critical enablers in the design and implementation of NBS. These tools allow for precise mapping, strategic planning, and effective monitoring of ecosystem-based projects, providing valuable data and insights to ensure the success of interventions. By integrating spatial data and remote sensing imagery, stakeholders can optimize NBS to address environmental challenges such as climate change, biodiversity loss, and urban resilience.

1. Mapping Ecosystems and Identifying Opportunities

Effective NBS projects begin with an in-depth understanding of the existing ecological landscape. GIS and remote sensing are instrumental in creating detailed maps and identifying potential areas for intervention.

a. Mapping Ecosystem Features

GIS enables the visualization of various ecosystem components, such as vegetation cover, water bodies, and soil types. By layering this data, stakeholders can gain a comprehensive understanding of the ecological features in a specific area. For instance, GIS can be used to map forests, wetlands, or coastal habitats, providing the baseline information needed for restoration or conservation projects.

b. Identifying Degraded Areas

Remote sensing technologies, such as satellite imagery and aerial drones, help detect areas experiencing environmental degradation. For example, satellite imagery can reveal deforestation patterns, soil erosion, or declining water quality, indicating where NBS interventions are most needed. This is particularly useful in large or inaccessible regions where on-the-ground assessments are challenging.

c. Understanding Spatial Relationships

GIS facilitates the analysis of spatial relationships between ecological features and human activities. For instance, mapping flood-prone areas alongside urban infrastructure can help identify sites where green infrastructure, such as rain gardens or wetlands, can mitigate flood risks. Similarly, GIS can highlight areas where reforestation efforts could enhance biodiversity corridors.

2. Planning and Designing NBS Interventions

Once potential sites for NBS have been identified, GIS and remote sensing play a pivotal role in designing interventions tailored to the specific needs and conditions of the area.

a. Scenario Modeling and Simulations

GIS allows for scenario modeling, which involves simulating the potential impacts of various NBS interventions under different conditions. For example, models can predict how planting mangroves along a coastline will reduce erosion or how constructing urban green roofs will mitigate heat islands. These simulations enable stakeholders to evaluate the effectiveness of proposed solutions before implementation.

b. Integrating Multidimensional Data

GIS integrates data from various sources, such as climate models, hydrological data, and socioeconomic factors. This multidimensional approach ensures that NBS designs are not only ecologically sound but also socially and economically viable. For example, incorporating climate projections into GIS analysis can help design wetlands that are resilient to future temperature and precipitation changes.

c. Optimizing Resource Allocation

GIS and remote sensing help optimize resource allocation by identifying priority areas for intervention. For instance, GIS can rank potential reforestation sites based on criteria such as carbon sequestration potential, biodiversity value, and proximity to vulnerable communities. This ensures that limited resources are directed to projects with the highest impact.

3. Monitoring and Managing NBS Projects

The success of NBS depends on continuous monitoring and adaptive management. GIS and remote sensing technologies provide the tools needed to track progress and make data-driven adjustments over time.

a. Monitoring Ecosystem Health

Remote sensing enables real-time monitoring of ecosystem health indicators, such as vegetation cover, water quality, and soil moisture levels. For instance, satellite imagery can be used to monitor the growth of reforested areas or the expansion of wetlands. These technologies provide regular updates, ensuring that NBS projects remain on track.

b. Detecting Changes and Trends

GIS allows stakeholders to analyze temporal changes in ecosystems by comparing historical and current data. For example, time-series analysis can reveal whether a wetland is expanding or shrinking, helping managers assess the effectiveness of restoration efforts. This capability is particularly valuable in detecting early signs of degradation or failure.

c. Supporting Adaptive Management

By combining monitoring data with predictive models, GIS and remote sensing support adaptive management strategies. For example, if a reforested area shows slower-than-expected growth due to water stress, GIS can identify nearby water sources for irrigation. Similarly, if urban green roofs are not reducing temperatures as anticipated, adjustments can be made to the vegetation mix or maintenance practices.

d. Enabling Large-Scale Monitoring

Remote sensing is especially beneficial for monitoring large-scale or remote NBS projects. For example, drones equipped with multispectral cameras can capture high-resolution images of coral reefs or mangroves, providing detailed insights that would be difficult to obtain through manual surveys. Similarly, satellite imagery can monitor deforestation or desertification across entire regions.

4. Examples of Applications

The integration of GIS and remote sensing into NBS has already demonstrated success across various applications:

• **Urban Resilience:** In cities, GIS is used to design green infrastructure that mitigates flooding and heat islands. For example, maps of stormwater flow can guide the placement of rain gardens and bioswales.

• **Coastal Protection:** Remote sensing has been instrumental in mapping mangroves and assessing their role in protecting coastlines from erosion and storm surges.

• **Agricultural Sustainability:** GIS and remote sensing help identify areas where agroforestry or soil conservation practices can enhance productivity and reduce environmental impacts.

• **Biodiversity Conservation:** Satellite imagery supports the monitoring of protected areas, detecting illegal activities such as logging or poaching.

5. Challenges and Considerations

While GIS and remote sensing offer significant benefits, their application in NBS also involves challenges:

• **Data Availability:** Access to high-resolution data can be limited, particularly in low-income regions.

• **Technical Expertise:** Implementing these technologies requires skilled professionals, which may not always be available in all contexts.

• **Costs:** The initial investment in GIS software, remote sensing equipment, and training can be a barrier for some projects.

• **Balancing Technology with Local Knowledge:** While these tools provide valuable insights, it is important to integrate them with local ecological knowledge to ensure culturally and ecologically appropriate solutions.

Applications of GIS and Remote Sensing in Urban Planning, Watershed Management, and Biodiversity Conservation

GIS and remote sensing technologies are integral to addressing complex environmental challenges and optimizing NBS. Their ability to collect, analyze, and visualize spatial data has made them essential tools in diverse fields, including urban planning, watershed management, and biodiversity conservation. These applications demonstrate the transformative potential of digital technologies in enhancing ecological outcomes and sustainability.

1. Urban Planning

Rapid urbanization poses significant challenges to cities, including pollution, heat islands, flooding, and loss of green spaces. GIS and remote sensing provide tools to integrate NBS into urban planning, making cities more resilient and sustainable.

a. Green Infrastructure Design

GIS enables the identification of optimal locations for urban green infrastructure, such as parks, green roofs, and vertical gardens. By mapping variables like population density, land use, and existing vegetation, planners can design spaces that maximize benefits such as air purification, cooling, and recreational opportunities. For instance, GIS can pinpoint areas most vulnerable to heat stress, guiding the placement of urban forests.

b. Stormwater Management

Cities face increasing flood risks due to impermeable surfaces and extreme weather events. Remote sensing and GIS help design stormwater management systems that mimic natural processes, such as rain gardens, bioswales, and constructed wetlands. For example, mapping stormwater flow paths using elevation data allows planners to identify areas where flooding can be mitigated through NBS.

c. Air Quality Improvement

GIS and remote sensing are used to monitor air pollution hotspots and assess how green infrastructure can mitigate pollution. By analyzing satellite imagery and ground-level data, planners can strategically plant vegetation to act as natural air filters, improving urban air quality and public health.

d. Urban Heat Island Mitigation

Satellite imagery helps identify urban heat islands, where temperatures are significantly higher due to dense infrastructure. GIS is then used to plan interventions such as tree planting, reflective surfaces, and green roofs to reduce heat, improve livability, and lower energy consumption.

e. Accessibility and Equity

GIS supports equitable urban planning by mapping underserved areas and ensuring that NBS projects are accessible to all residents. For instance, green spaces can be planned to provide recreational opportunities in low-income neighborhoods, promoting social equity.

2. Watershed Management

Healthy watersheds are critical for water supply, flood control, and ecosystem health. GIS and remote sensing play a vital role in watershed management, guiding interventions that restore and protect these critical ecosystems.

a. Watershed Mapping and Analysis

GIS allows for detailed mapping of watersheds, including their boundaries, topography, and hydrological features. By integrating remote sensing data, such as rainfall patterns and vegetation cover, planners can identify areas prone to erosion, sedimentation, or pollution.

b. Riparian Zone Restoration

Remote sensing helps identify degraded riparian zones that require restoration. By analyzing vegetation cover along waterways, GIS can prioritize areas for planting riparian buffers, which improve water quality, reduce erosion, and enhance habitat connectivity.

c. Flood Risk Assessment

Flooding is a major challenge in watersheds, especially during extreme weather events. GIS and remote sensing technologies help model flood risks by integrating rainfall data, soil permeability, and topography. These insights guide the implementation of NBS, such as reforestation, wetlands restoration, and floodplain reconnection, to mitigate flooding.

d. Water Quality Monitoring

Remote sensing technologies, such as satellite imagery and drones, monitor water quality indicators, including turbidity, temperature, and nutrient levels. GIS integrates this data to identify pollution sources and design interventions such as buffer strips or constructed wetlands to filter runoff and reduce contaminants.

e. Sustainable Land Use Planning

GIS helps manage land use within watersheds to balance ecological health and human needs. For example, it can identify areas suitable for agroforestry or contour farming, which reduce runoff and enhance soil health, contributing to overall watershed resilience.

3. Biodiversity Conservation

Biodiversity underpins ecosystem services and global ecological stability, but it is under severe threat from habitat loss, climate change, and human activities. GIS and remote sensing technologies provide critical tools for conserving biodiversity through NBS.

a. Habitat Mapping and Prioritization

GIS and remote sensing are used to map habitats, assess their health, and identify areas requiring conservation or restoration. For instance, satellite imagery can detect deforestation or changes in wetland areas, allowing conservationists to prioritize reforestation or wetland restoration projects.

b. Wildlife Corridor Design

Fragmentation of habitats due to human activity is a significant threat to biodiversity. GIS enables the design of wildlife corridors by identifying key habitat patches and the most suitable pathways to connect them. These corridors support species migration, breeding, and genetic diversity.

c. Monitoring Ecosystem Health

Remote sensing technologies track changes in ecosystems, such as vegetation loss, water availability, or land degradation. These tools provide real-time data that can inform adaptive management strategies to maintain or restore ecosystem health.

d. Climate Change Adaptation

GIS and remote sensing are essential for designing biodiversity-focused NBS that address climate change. For example, they can identify areas suitable for mangrove restoration, which not only protect coastlines from storm surges but also provide critical habitats for marine species.

e. Protected Area Management

GIS supports the management of protected areas by mapping boundaries, monitoring human activities, and assessing ecological conditions. For example, drones can detect illegal logging or poaching, while satellite imagery monitors deforestation within protected forests.

f. Species Distribution Modeling

GIS integrates ecological data with environmental variables to predict species distributions under current and future conditions. This information guides conservation efforts, such as habitat restoration or the establishment of new protected areas, to ensure the survival of vulnerable species.

Challenges and Opportunities in Scaling GIS and Remote Sensing for Nature-Based Solutions

GIS and remote sensing have proven instrumental in advancing NBS through their ability to collect, analyze, and visualize spatial and environmental data. However, the scalability of these technologies to broader contexts and larger projects comes with both challenges and opportunities. This section explores the key barriers to scaling GIS and remote sensing for NBS while highlighting opportunities for their broader implementation to optimize ecosystem management and sustainability efforts.

Challenges in Scaling GIS and Remote Sensing for NBS

Despite their transformative potential, several challenges hinder the widespread adoption and scalability of GIS and remote sensing technologies in NBS projects.

1. Limited Data Accessibility and Quality

• High-Resolution Data Availability:

Many NBS projects, particularly in low-income regions, lack access to high-resolution data necessary for precise mapping and monitoring. This limits the ability to tailor solutions to specific ecological conditions.

• Data Gaps in Remote Areas:

Remote and underdeveloped regions often lack sufficient satellite imagery or ground-based validation data, making it difficult to analyze ecosystem conditions accurately.

• Temporal Gaps:

Inconsistent data collection over time can hinder the ability to monitor changes or trends in ecosystems, reducing the effectiveness of long-term NBS management.

2. High Costs of Technology and Expertise

• Cost of Tools and Software:

Advanced GIS software and high-resolution satellite imagery can be prohibitively expensive for smaller organizations and projects.

• Specialized Training Requirements:

Implementing GIS and remote sensing requires skilled professionals to interpret data and operate tools, which may not be readily available in all regions.

3. Technological Infrastructure

• Digital Divide:

Many developing countries lack the infrastructure, such as reliable internet and computing power, needed to process large datasets generated by GIS and remote sensing technologies.

• Compatibility Issues:

Integrating diverse data sources, including satellite imagery, IoT sensors, and local databases, can pose technical challenges, particularly when using older or proprietary systems.

4. Ethical and Social Concerns

• Data Privacy:

Using GIS and remote sensing often involves collecting sensitive spatial data, such as land use patterns or community information, raising privacy concerns.

• Equity in Access:

Disparities in access to technology and data may exacerbate inequalities, excluding marginalized communities from participating in NBS planning and decision-making.

5. Environmental and Technological Sensitivity

• Accuracy in Dynamic Environments:

Ecosystems are inherently dynamic, and satellite or drone-based data may not always capture real-time changes, leading to inaccuracies.

• Over-Reliance on Technology:

Excessive dependence on GIS and remote sensing risks neglecting local ecological knowledge and on-the-ground insights, which are essential for sustainable NBS implementation.

Opportunities in Scaling GIS and Remote Sensing for NBS

While challenges exist, there are significant opportunities to overcome these barriers and scale GIS and remote sensing for more effective and widespread application in NBS.

1. Advancements in Technology

• Improved Satellite Imagery:

Advances in satellite technology, such as higher resolution and increased revisit frequency, provide more accurate and detailed data.

For instance, initiatives like Sentinel (EU) and Landsat (US) offer open-access satellite data that can be used for NBS.

• Drones and UAVs:

Unmanned Aerial Vehicles (UAVs) or drones offer cost-effective and high-resolution imaging solutions for monitoring ecosystems, especially in remote or small-scale projects.

• Machine Learning and AI Integration:

Artificial intelligence and machine learning can process large datasets efficiently, extracting actionable insights from complex spatial data for better decision-making in NBS projects.

2. Open Data Initiatives

• Global Data Sharing:

Open data platforms, such as Google Earth Engine and the Copernicus Open Access Hub, provide free access to satellite imagery and analytical tools, democratizing the use of GIS and remote sensing for NBS.

• Collaborative Projects:

International collaborations, such as the Global Forest Watch, make it easier to monitor ecosystems and biodiversity across regions, fostering global efforts in conservation and restoration.

3. Lower Costs and Increased Accessibility

• Affordable Technologies:

The decreasing costs of hardware, such as drones and IoT sensors, make GIS and remote sensing more accessible to small-scale projects and developing regions.

• **Cloud Computing:**

Cloud-based GIS platforms reduce the need for expensive local infrastructure, enabling users to process and analyze large datasets remotely.

4. Enhanced Stakeholder Engagement

• **Participatory GIS:**

Community-based mapping tools enable local populations to contribute to NBS projects by sharing data and insights, fostering inclusivity and empowering stakeholders.

• **Education and Capacity Building:**

Investments in training programs and knowledge-sharing platforms can build local expertise in GIS and remote sensing, enhancing the capacity of communities and organizations to implement NBS.

5. Policy Support and Funding

• **Government and Donor Support:**

Policymakers and funding agencies are increasingly recognizing the value of GIS and remote sensing in achieving sustainability goals. Funding for capacity-building initiatives can address cost and expertise barriers.

• **Incentives for Open Innovation:**

Governments and private entities can incentivize the development of open-source GIS tools, fostering innovation and reducing costs for users.

6. Integration with Other Technologies

• IoT and Big Data:

Combining GIS with IoT devices enables real-time monitoring of ecosystems, enhancing the accuracy and responsiveness of NBS.

• Digital Twins:

Digital twin technology, which creates virtual models of ecosystems, allows for the testing and optimization of NBS designs before implementation, reducing risks and improving outcomes.

Addressing Challenges for Scalable Opportunities

To fully capitalize on these opportunities, targeted efforts must be made to address the challenges of scaling GIS and remote sensing for NBS:

• **Investment in Capacity Building:** Training programs, particularly in developing regions, are essential to bridge the skill gap and empower local stakeholders.

• **Promoting Data Sharing:** Global partnerships and open-data initiatives can enhance access to high-quality spatial data, particularly for underserved regions.

• **Fostering Collaboration:** Multi-stakeholder approaches that involve governments, NGOs, academia, and the private sector can pool resources and expertise, ensuring scalable and equitable solutions.

• **Developing Cost-Effective Solutions:** Encouraging innovation in low-cost tools and software can make GIS and remote sensing technologies more accessible to a broader audience.

Chapter 3: The Internet of Things for Monitoring and Maintenance

The IoT is revolutionizing how we monitor and manage NBS. By connecting physical devices such as sensors, cameras, and weather stations to digital networks, IoT enables real-time data collection and analysis, providing unprecedented insights into ecosystem health and functionality. This technology plays a critical role in ensuring the success of NBS by facilitating predictive maintenance, adaptive management, and efficient resource allocation.

This chapter explores the applications of IoT in NBS, focusing on how sensors and connected devices track key environmental parameters, such as water quality, soil health, and air pollution. It also examines the role of IoT in optimizing the performance of NBS through predictive analytics and remote monitoring, ensuring that interventions remain effective and sustainable over time. Finally, the chapter addresses the challenges and opportunities of integrating IoT into NBS projects, offering insights into its potential to enhance the resilience and scalability of nature-based approaches.

IoT Applications in Real-Time Monitoring of Ecosystems and Environmental Conditions

The IoT has emerged as a transformative technology for real-time monitoring of ecosystems and environmental conditions, providing actionable insights to support the implementation and management of NBS. By connecting sensors, devices, and networks, IoT enables the continuous collection, transmission, and analysis of environmental data. This capability is crucial for monitoring ecosystem health, identifying emerging threats, and ensuring that NBS interventions are functioning as intended.

1. Real-Time Data Collection

IoT enables the deployment of sensor networks that collect data on a wide range of environmental parameters. These sensors are strategically placed in ecosystems to provide a detailed understanding of their dynamics.

a. Monitoring Water Quality

Water quality is a critical indicator of ecosystem health, particularly in wetlands, rivers, and coastal environments. IoT sensors can monitor parameters such as pH, dissolved oxygen, turbidity, and nutrient levels in real time. For example:

• In wetlands, IoT devices can detect nutrient imbalances caused by agricultural runoff, helping managers address potential eutrophication before it escalates.

• Coastal sensors can monitor salinity and temperature, providing early warnings of conditions that could harm marine life, such as coral bleaching events.

b. Tracking Soil Conditions

Healthy soil is essential for agriculture, reforestation, and ecosystem restoration. IoT sensors measure soil moisture, temperature, and nutrient levels, enabling adaptive management of NBS projects. For instance:

• In agroforestry systems, soil moisture sensors guide irrigation schedules, ensuring that water resources are used efficiently.

• In reforestation projects, these sensors can track soil health, helping managers determine whether conditions are suitable for tree growth.

c. Measuring Air Quality

Air quality monitoring is vital for urban green infrastructure projects. IoT-enabled devices track pollutants such as carbon dioxide (CO_2), nitrogen dioxide (NO_2), and particulate matter (PM2.5), providing data that informs the placement and maintenance of green spaces. For example:

• IoT networks in cities can measure how well urban forests and green roofs are reducing air pollution levels.

• Real-time air quality data can guide community decisions on expanding vegetation in high-pollution areas.

2. Enhancing Ecosystem Health Assessments

IoT systems improve ecosystem health assessments by integrating data from multiple sensors, providing a comprehensive view of environmental conditions.

a. Detecting Changes in Biodiversity

IoT devices, such as acoustic sensors and camera traps, monitor wildlife activity in forests, wetlands, and marine environments. These technologies help track changes in biodiversity and detect the presence of invasive species. For example:

• Acoustic sensors in forests can record bird calls and insect activity, offering insights into ecosystem health and biodiversity trends.

• Camera traps equipped with IoT connectivity can detect the movement of endangered species, providing data for conservation planning.

b. Monitoring Vegetation Dynamics

IoT sensors track vegetation growth and health in real time, enabling proactive management of reforestation and urban green infrastructure projects. For example:

• In reforested areas, sensors can measure tree canopy coverage and leaf area index, ensuring that growth targets are met.

• IoT devices can also monitor vegetation stress caused by drought, pests, or disease, prompting timely interventions.

3. Supporting Disaster Risk Reduction

IoT technologies are particularly valuable for monitoring and mitigating environmental risks, such as floods, wildfires, and storms, which can threaten ecosystems and communities.

a. Flood Monitoring

IoT-enabled sensors track water levels in rivers, reservoirs, and wetlands, providing early warnings of potential flooding. For instance:

• In wetlands designed for flood control, water level sensors detect rising levels and alert managers to take preventive measures.

• IoT systems in urban areas monitor stormwater drainage systems, ensuring that rain gardens and bioswales are functioning effectively during heavy rainfall.

b. Wildfire Detection

IoT networks are deployed in forests and grasslands to detect early signs of wildfires, such as increased temperature, smoke, or sudden drops in humidity. For example:

• Temperature and humidity sensors can signal conditions that are conducive to wildfires, enabling authorities to implement mitigation strategies.

• Smoke detectors in IoT networks can identify fires at their inception, minimizing damage to ecosystems and nearby communities.

c. Storm Monitoring

IoT weather stations collect data on wind speed, precipitation, and temperature, providing early warnings of extreme weather events. These systems help managers prepare NBS projects, such as coastal mangroves or urban green spaces, to withstand storms and protect surrounding areas.

4. Facilitating Adaptive Management

IoT systems enable adaptive management by providing continuous feedback on the performance of NBS interventions. This data-driven approach ensures that projects remain effective under changing environmental conditions.

a. Continuous Monitoring and Adjustments

Real-time data from IoT sensors allows managers to identify and address issues as they arise. For example:

• In constructed wetlands, water flow sensors can detect blockages or irregularities, prompting immediate maintenance.

• In urban green infrastructure, temperature and moisture sensors can guide irrigation and pruning schedules to optimize plant health.

b. Integration with Predictive Analytics

IoT data is often integrated with predictive analytics tools, such as machine learning models, to forecast ecosystem changes and plan proactive interventions. For instance:

• Predictive models based on IoT data can identify areas at risk of drought, guiding the expansion of irrigation systems or the planting of drought-tolerant species.

• In urban areas, IoT-enabled traffic sensors can assess the effectiveness of green corridors in reducing heat islands and improving air quality.

5. Challenges and Opportunities

While IoT offers significant advantages, its implementation in NBS comes with challenges and opportunities:

Challenges

• **Cost and Accessibility:** IoT sensors and networks can be expensive, limiting their adoption in resource-constrained regions.

• **Data Overload:** Managing and analyzing the vast amount of data generated by IoT systems requires robust infrastructure and expertise.

• **Technological Limitations:** IoT devices may face connectivity issues in remote areas or harsh environmental conditions.

Opportunities

• **Scalability:** Advances in IoT technology, such as low-cost sensors and wireless networks, make it increasingly scalable for large NBS projects.

• **Integration with Other Technologies:** IoT can be combined with GIS, remote sensing, and blockchain to create comprehensive monitoring systems.

• **Citizen Engagement:** IoT data can be shared with communities, fostering transparency and collaboration in NBS management.

Use of Sensors for Tracking Water Quality, Soil Health, and Air Pollution in Nature-Based Solutions

The effective implementation and monitoring of NBS require accurate and continuous data on environmental conditions. Sensors play a pivotal role in tracking critical indicators such as water quality, soil health, and air pollution, ensuring that NBS interventions meet their intended goals. By providing real-time data, these sensors enable proactive management, inform decision-making, and enhance the performance and scalability of NBS projects.

1. Tracking Water Quality

Water quality is a fundamental indicator of ecosystem health, particularly in aquatic and riparian environments. Sensors provide essential data for monitoring water conditions and ensuring the success of NBS interventions aimed at improving water quality and availability.

a. Key Parameters Monitored

• **pH Levels:** Sensors measure the acidity or alkalinity of water, critical for maintaining aquatic biodiversity. For instance, wetlands restored as part of NBS projects require stable pH levels to support vegetation and aquatic species.

• **Dissolved Oxygen (DO):** Monitoring DO levels ensures that aquatic habitats remain conducive to fish and other organisms.

Reduced oxygen levels can indicate pollution or eutrophication, requiring intervention.

• **Turbidity and Sedimentation:** Turbidity sensors track water clarity, which is essential for detecting erosion or runoff affecting aquatic ecosystems.

• **Nutrient Levels:** Sensors measure concentrations of nitrogen, phosphorus, and other nutrients that can lead to algal blooms and water quality degradation.

b. Applications in NBS

• **Wetland Restoration:** Sensors installed in constructed or restored wetlands monitor water quality parameters, ensuring that these ecosystems filter pollutants effectively.

• **Urban Stormwater Management:** Rain gardens and bioswales designed to manage stormwater runoff use sensors to track nutrient levels and ensure pollutant removal.

• **Riparian Buffers:** In agricultural landscapes, sensors monitor water quality in streams adjacent to riparian buffers, measuring the effectiveness of these NBS in reducing nutrient runoff.

c. Benefits of Real-Time Monitoring

Real-time water quality monitoring enables rapid responses to emerging issues, such as pollution spikes or changes in water chemistry. This ensures that NBS interventions remain effective and adaptable to changing conditions.

2. Monitoring Soil Health

Healthy soils are vital for the success of NBS, particularly in agricultural, reforestation, and urban green infrastructure projects. Sensors provide detailed insights into soil conditions, enabling informed decisions about management practices.

a. Key Parameters Monitored

• **Soil Moisture:** Sensors measure moisture levels to ensure optimal hydration for vegetation. In dry regions, this data helps guide irrigation schedules for agroforestry or reforestation projects.

• **Soil Temperature:** Monitoring soil temperature supports the health of plants and microbial communities. For instance, sensors detect temperature fluctuations that may affect seed germination or root development.

• **Nutrient Content:** Sensors track levels of essential nutrients like nitrogen, phosphorus, and potassium, ensuring that soils remain fertile for vegetation growth.

• **Soil Compaction:** Measuring soil density helps assess whether compaction is hindering root growth or water infiltration.

b. Applications in NBS

• **Reforestation Projects:** Soil sensors monitor the health of reforested areas, ensuring that trees have the moisture and nutrients needed to thrive.

• **Urban Green Infrastructure:** In urban settings, sensors track soil conditions in green roofs, parks, and vertical gardens, optimizing their performance in reducing heat and improving air quality.

• **Agroforestry Systems:** Sensors monitor soil health in mixed-use landscapes, helping balance agricultural productivity with ecosystem restoration.

c. Enhancing Adaptive Management

By providing real-time data on soil conditions, sensors support adaptive management strategies. For example, if soil moisture levels drop below optimal thresholds, managers can adjust irrigation schedules or introduce drought-tolerant plant species.

3. Measuring Air Pollution

Air pollution poses significant challenges to human health and environmental sustainability. Sensors are critical for monitoring air quality and assessing the effectiveness of NBS interventions aimed at reducing pollution.

a. Key Pollutants Monitored

• **Particulate Matter (PM2.5 and PM10):** Sensors measure airborne particles that affect air quality and respiratory health. These measurements are crucial for evaluating the impact of urban green infrastructure, such as tree planting or green walls.

• **CO_2:** Monitoring CO_2 levels helps assess the role of NBS in carbon sequestration and climate mitigation efforts.

• **NO_2 :** Sensors track NO_2 levels, a common pollutant from vehicle emissions, to evaluate the effectiveness of green corridors in urban areas.

• **Ozone (O_3):** Monitoring ozone concentrations provides insights into the air quality benefits of vegetation, which can absorb ozone and other pollutants.

b. Applications in NBS

• **Urban Forests:** Sensors monitor air quality improvements in areas with dense tree planting, quantifying the role of urban forests in reducing pollutants.

• **Green Walls and Roofs:** Air quality sensors installed near green walls or roofs measure their effectiveness in filtering pollutants and cooling urban environments.

• **Traffic Corridors:** Sensors along green corridors track reductions in vehicle emissions, demonstrating the effectiveness of these NBS in improving air quality for nearby residents.

c. Supporting Public Health Goals

By providing detailed data on air quality, sensors enable NBS projects to align with public health objectives. For example, reducing particulate matter and NO_2 levels in urban areas improves respiratory health and reduces the burden of air pollution-related diseases.

4. Challenges and Opportunities

While sensors offer significant advantages for tracking water quality, soil health, and air pollution, their use in NBS also presents challenges and opportunities.

Challenges

• **Cost:** High-quality sensors and their maintenance can be expensive, limiting their deployment in resource-constrained regions.

• **Connectivity Issues:** Remote areas often lack reliable internet or communication networks to transmit sensor data in real time.

• **Data Overload:** Managing and interpreting large volumes of data generated by sensors requires robust infrastructure and technical expertise.

Opportunities

• **Advances in Sensor Technology:** The development of low-cost, durable sensors makes real-time monitoring more accessible for NBS projects worldwide.

• **Integration with Other Technologies:** Combining sensors with IoT, GIS, and remote sensing enhances the effectiveness of NBS monitoring systems.

• **Citizen Science:** Engaging communities in sensor deployment and data collection fosters local involvement and ensures that NBS projects address community needs.

Insights on How IoT Enables Predictive Maintenance and Adaptive Management of Nature-Based Solutions

The IoT has transformed the way ecosystems and NBS are managed. By integrating sensors, networks, and data analytics, IoT enables continuous monitoring, real-time insights, and predictive capabilities that support both maintenance and adaptive management. These capabilities ensure that NBS remain effective and resilient over time, addressing challenges proactively and optimizing performance.

1. Predictive Maintenance in NBS

Predictive maintenance involves anticipating potential issues in infrastructure or ecosystems before they escalate, reducing downtime and resource waste. IoT plays a critical role in enabling this by providing data-driven insights into the condition of NBS.

a. Real-Time Condition Monitoring

IoT devices continuously monitor environmental parameters, providing early warnings of issues that could compromise the performance of NBS. For instance:

• **Green Roofs and Walls:** Sensors measure soil moisture, temperature, and vegetation health, alerting managers to irrigation needs or vegetation stress.

• **Constructed Wetlands:** Water flow and quality sensors detect blockages, sediment buildup, or changes in nutrient levels that could affect filtration efficiency.

b. Identifying Anomalies

IoT systems equipped with machine learning algorithms can identify anomalies in ecosystem data. For example:

• In urban stormwater systems, flow sensors detect irregularities in water movement, signaling clogged bioswales or rain gardens.

• In reforested areas, soil and temperature sensors identify areas where tree growth is lagging, suggesting localized issues such as pests or nutrient deficiencies.

c. Proactive Repairs and Adjustments

IoT data supports timely interventions to address emerging problems. For example:

• If a wetland sensor indicates sediment accumulation, managers can schedule maintenance to prevent clogging.

• In agricultural NBS, moisture sensors guide targeted irrigation, preventing water stress and improving productivity.

2. Adaptive Management in NBS

Adaptive management involves continuously adjusting strategies to respond to changing conditions or new information. IoT enables this approach by providing dynamic, real-time data that informs decision-making and enhances resilience.

a. Dynamic Response to Environmental Changes

IoT systems allow NBS to respond effectively to environmental fluctuations. For example:

• **Flood Management:** Sensors in river basins monitor water levels during storms, enabling managers to adjust floodplain designs or implement temporary barriers to mitigate risks.

• **Drought Resilience:** Soil moisture sensors in agroforestry systems help optimize irrigation schedules, ensuring that water resources are allocated efficiently during droughts.

b. Continuous Feedback Loops

IoT facilitates feedback loops that connect monitoring with action. For instance:

• In urban green spaces, air quality sensors measure pollutant levels, guiding the placement of additional vegetation to maximize filtration benefits.

• In coastal mangrove restoration projects, salinity sensors track water conditions, helping managers adapt planting strategies to ensure seedling survival.

c. Data-Driven Decision Making

IoT systems generate comprehensive datasets that inform strategic decisions. For example:

• In watershed management, IoT data on rainfall, runoff, and water quality enables adaptive strategies to balance agricultural needs with ecosystem health.

• In urban areas, IoT-based heat sensors help optimize the placement of green roofs and shaded corridors to mitigate urban heat islands.

3. Use Cases of IoT in Predictive Maintenance and Adaptive Management

IoT has been successfully applied in various contexts to enhance the performance and resilience of NBS. Key examples include:

a. Wetland Restoration

• IoT sensors monitor water quality and flow rates in wetlands, enabling predictive maintenance of filtration systems.

• Data on vegetation health guides adaptive strategies for planting or invasive species management.

b. Urban Green Infrastructure

• Green roofs and walls equipped with IoT sensors track moisture levels, ensuring vegetation remains healthy and effective in filtering pollutants.

• IoT-based air quality sensors measure the impact of green corridors, guiding their expansion or redesign.

c. Reforestation Projects

• Soil and climate sensors in reforested areas provide data on growth conditions, helping managers adjust planting density or species selection.

• Predictive analytics based on IoT data forecast the impact of pests or diseases, enabling proactive responses.

d. Coastal Ecosystems

• Mangrove restoration projects use IoT devices to monitor tidal patterns, salinity, and sediment deposition, ensuring optimal conditions for growth.

• Sensors track storm impacts, guiding adaptive measures to enhance coastal protection.

4. Benefits of IoT in Maintenance and Management

The integration of IoT into NBS offers several advantages for predictive maintenance and adaptive management:

a. Cost Efficiency

• Predictive maintenance reduces the need for costly repairs by addressing issues early.

• Optimized resource use, such as targeted irrigation or sediment removal, minimizes waste.

b. Improved Effectiveness

• Real-time data ensures that NBS are functioning as intended, maximizing their environmental and societal benefits.

• Adaptive management strategies keep NBS resilient in the face of changing conditions, such as climate variability or urban development.

c. Scalability

• IoT systems enable large-scale monitoring, making it easier to replicate successful NBS projects in new locations.

• Integration with other digital technologies, such as GIS and remote sensing, enhances the scalability of IoT applications.

5. Challenges and Future Opportunities

While IoT has significant potential, there are challenges to its widespread adoption in NBS:

Challenges

• **Cost:** The installation and maintenance of IoT systems can be expensive, particularly in resource-limited regions.

• **Connectivity:** Reliable internet and power infrastructure are needed to support IoT networks, which may be lacking in remote areas.

• **Data Management:** Managing and interpreting large volumes of IoT-generated data requires specialized expertise and robust systems.

Opportunities

• **Advances in IoT Technology:** The development of low-cost, energy-efficient sensors makes IoT more accessible for NBS projects.

• **Integration with Predictive Analytics:** Combining IoT data with machine learning enhances predictive capabilities, improving maintenance and management strategies.

• **Citizen Science and Engagement:** IoT systems can involve local communities in data collection and monitoring, fostering greater ownership and collaboration in NBS efforts.

Chapter 4: Artificial Intelligence and Machine Learning for Optimized Nature-Based Solutions

AI and Machine Learning (ML) are transforming how NBS are designed, implemented, and monitored. By processing vast amounts of environmental data, these technologies offer insights into complex ecosystem dynamics, enabling smarter, more efficient solutions. From predictive modeling of climate impacts to optimizing resource allocation, AI and ML enhance the precision and adaptability of NBS projects.

This chapter explores the applications of AI and ML in NBS, including their use in analyzing environmental data, predicting ecosystem responses, and improving decision-making processes. It highlights their potential to optimize interventions, reduce costs, and enhance scalability while addressing challenges such as data accessibility and ethical considerations. By leveraging AI and ML, NBS can achieve greater impact and resilience in tackling global sustainability challenges.

Leveraging AI to Analyze Complex Environmental Data and Predict Ecosystem Behavior

AI has emerged as a powerful tool for analyzing complex environmental data and predicting ecosystem behavior, offering transformative potential for NBS. As ecosystems are inherently dynamic and influenced by numerous variables, understanding their behavior requires sophisticated analytical tools. AI's ability to process vast amounts of data, identify patterns, and generate predictive models allows for more effective planning, implementation, and management of NBS.

1. The Role of AI in Environmental Data Analysis

AI's capacity to handle large and diverse datasets enables a deeper understanding of environmental systems. By integrating information from multiple sources, AI identifies patterns and relationships that would be difficult or impossible to discern using traditional methods.

a. Integrating Multisource Data

Environmental data often comes from various sources, including satellite imagery, IoT sensors, and field surveys. AI algorithms can process and synthesize this data to provide a comprehensive picture of ecosystem health. For example:

• Satellite data on land use can be combined with weather patterns to assess the impacts of deforestation on regional climates.

• IoT sensors tracking soil moisture, temperature, and nutrient levels can be analyzed alongside remote sensing data to monitor agricultural landscapes.

b. Identifying Patterns and Trends

AI techniques, such as ML, excel at recognizing patterns and trends in large datasets. For instance:

• In urban green infrastructure projects, AI can analyze historical temperature and pollution data to identify areas most in need of cooling or air purification.

• In coastal ecosystems, AI can detect patterns in sediment deposition and erosion, guiding mangrove restoration efforts.

c. Real-Time Data Processing

AI systems can analyze data in real time, enabling immediate insights and responses. For example:

• In wetlands designed for flood mitigation, AI algorithms can process real-time water level data to predict flooding risks and guide adaptive management.

• AI-powered drones can analyze vegetation health during reforestation projects, identifying stressed areas requiring intervention.

2. Predicting Ecosystem Behavior with AI

AI models can simulate ecosystem behavior under different conditions, providing valuable insights for planning and decision-making in NBS projects. These predictions help stakeholders anticipate challenges, optimize interventions, and achieve desired outcomes.

a. Climate Impact Modeling

AI-powered climate models predict how ecosystems will respond to changing temperatures, precipitation patterns, and extreme weather events. For example:

• AI simulations can forecast how rising sea levels will affect coastal habitats, guiding the placement of protective mangroves or living shorelines.

• In urban areas, AI models predict the cooling effects of green roofs under various climate scenarios, helping planners prioritize their installation.

b. Biodiversity and Habitat Predictions

AI tools can analyze species distribution and habitat conditions to predict the impacts of environmental changes on biodiversity. For instance:

• AI models forecast how habitat fragmentation affects species migration, guiding the design of wildlife corridors.

• Predictive models assess the potential spread of invasive species, enabling proactive measures to protect native biodiversity.

c. Ecosystem Services Evaluation

AI systems evaluate the benefits provided by ecosystems, such as carbon sequestration, water filtration, and flood regulation. For example:

• In agricultural landscapes, AI predicts the soil carbon sequestration potential of agroforestry systems under different management practices.

• AI models estimate the water filtration capacity of restored wetlands, supporting decisions on their design and scale.

d. Early Warning Systems

AI-driven early warning systems predict environmental risks, such as droughts, floods, or wildfires. These systems enable proactive management of NBS to mitigate impacts. For example:

• In watersheds, AI models analyze rainfall and runoff data to predict flash floods, guiding the deployment of floodplain reconnection projects.

• AI-powered fire detection systems monitor forest conditions, predicting areas at high risk of wildfires and informing preventative measures.

3. Applications in NBS Projects

AI's ability to analyze complex environmental data and predict ecosystem behavior has been applied successfully in various NBS contexts:

a. Urban Green Infrastructure

In cities, AI models help optimize the placement of green spaces, such as parks, green roofs, and urban forests. By analyzing urban heat islands, traffic patterns, and air quality data, AI ensures that interventions maximize cooling, pollution reduction, and public accessibility.

b. Wetland Restoration

AI systems analyze hydrological data to design wetlands that effectively manage stormwater, improve water quality, and support biodiversity. Predictive models simulate wetland performance under different rainfall scenarios, ensuring their resilience to climate variability.

c. Coastal Protection

In coastal areas, AI tools guide the restoration of mangroves, seagrasses, and coral reefs by analyzing factors such as tidal patterns, sediment transport, and water quality. Predictive models estimate the protective benefits of these ecosystems against storm surges and erosion.

d. Reforestation and Agroforestry

AI algorithms optimize tree planting strategies by analyzing soil conditions, climate data, and species compatibility. Predictive models assess the long-term benefits of reforestation for carbon sequestration, biodiversity, and community livelihoods.

4. Challenges in Leveraging AI for NBS

While AI offers significant benefits, its application in NBS is not without challenges:

a. Data Quality and Availability

AI models rely on high-quality data, which may be limited in certain regions or ecosystems. Incomplete or inaccurate datasets can compromise the reliability of predictions.

b. Technical Expertise

Developing and deploying AI models require specialized knowledge and skills, which may not be readily available in all contexts. Building local capacity is essential for scaling AI applications in NBS.

c. Cost and Infrastructure

AI systems can be resource-intensive, requiring substantial computational power and financial investment. Ensuring accessibility for small-scale projects and developing regions is a key challenge.

d. Ethical Considerations

AI applications must address ethical concerns, such as data privacy, algorithm bias, and the potential for misuse of predictive models.

5. Opportunities for Advancing AI in NBS

Despite these challenges, advancements in AI and data science present opportunities to enhance its role in NBS:

a. Open-Source Platforms

Open-source AI tools and datasets democratize access, enabling broader adoption of AI in NBS projects.

b. Integration with Other Technologies

Combining AI with IoT, GIS, and remote sensing enhances the accuracy and scalability of environmental data analysis and predictions.

c. Citizen Science and Community Involvement

Engaging local communities in data collection and validation can improve the quality and relevance of AI models while fostering collaboration and ownership.

d. Continuous Learning

AI systems that incorporate feedback loops can improve their accuracy over time, adapting to new data and evolving ecosystem dynamics.

Machine Learning Models for Optimizing Resource Allocation and Assessing Risks

ML models have become invaluable tools in the management and optimization of NBS. By analyzing large datasets and uncovering patterns, these models enhance decision-making by providing insights into resource allocation and risk assessment. ML's ability to adapt and improve over time ensures that NBS remain efficient, sustainable, and resilient in the face of dynamic environmental and social conditions.

1. Optimizing Resource Allocation

Resource allocation is a critical aspect of designing and implementing NBS. ML models improve the precision and efficiency of resource use, ensuring that investments yield maximum environmental and societal benefits.

a. Prioritizing Sites for NBS Implementation

ML algorithms analyze spatial and ecological data to identify areas where NBS interventions will have the greatest impact. For example:

• **Urban Green Infrastructure:** ML models can prioritize locations for green roofs or parks by analyzing data on urban heat islands, population density, and air pollution levels.

• **Reforestation Projects:** ML algorithms assess soil quality, precipitation patterns, and biodiversity hotspots to identify optimal areas for planting trees.

b. Optimizing Water Use in NBS

In water-scarce regions, ML models play a key role in managing water resources for NBS:

• **Irrigation Optimization:** ML systems use data from IoT sensors to predict soil moisture levels and schedule irrigation for agroforestry or green infrastructure, reducing water waste.

• **Floodplain Management:** Models analyze hydrological data to determine how much water to retain or release in floodplains, ensuring effective flood mitigation and ecosystem health.

c. Cost-Effective Allocation of Financial Resources

ML models evaluate the cost-effectiveness of various NBS interventions, helping stakeholders allocate budgets efficiently:

• By analyzing historical data and projected outcomes, ML systems rank potential projects based on their environmental, economic, and social returns on investment.

• These insights ensure that limited financial resources are directed to interventions with the highest impact.

2. Assessing Environmental and Operational Risks

Accurately assessing risks is crucial for the long-term success of NBS. ML models excel in predicting potential threats and providing early warnings, enabling stakeholders to mitigate risks proactively.

a. Predicting Climate-Related Risks

ML models analyze historical and real-time climate data to predict risks such as droughts, floods, or extreme temperatures. For example:

• **Drought Risk Assessment:** ML algorithms identify regions vulnerable to water scarcity, guiding the implementation of drought-resilient NBS like xeriscaping or rainwater harvesting.

• **Flood Prediction:** By analyzing rainfall patterns, river flow data, and topography, ML models forecast flood events, informing the design and management of wetlands and floodplains.

b. Monitoring and Managing Ecosystem Health

ML systems assess ecosystem health by detecting early signs of degradation or imbalance. For instance:

• **Forest Health Monitoring:** ML models analyze satellite imagery and IoT sensor data to identify tree stress caused by pests, disease, or environmental changes.

• **Wetland Dynamics:** Algorithms track changes in water quality and vegetation cover in wetlands, providing insights into potential threats like eutrophication or invasive species.

c. Evaluating Social and Economic Risks

ML models incorporate socioeconomic data to assess risks that may affect the success of NBS projects. For example:

• In urban areas, ML systems evaluate the likelihood of community resistance to green infrastructure projects based on historical data and public sentiment analysis.

• For rural NBS, ML algorithms assess risks associated with competing land uses, such as agriculture or development, and recommend strategies to balance interests.

3. Enhancing Decision-Making with ML Models

ML models provide actionable insights that improve decision-making at every stage of NBS implementation, from planning to long-term management.

a. Scenario Modeling

ML-powered simulations predict how ecosystems will respond to different management strategies or environmental changes. For example:

• In agroforestry systems, ML models simulate how various planting patterns will impact crop yields, biodiversity, and carbon sequestration.

• For coastal restoration, ML algorithms predict the effectiveness of mangroves in mitigating storm surges under different climate scenarios.

b. Adaptive Management

ML systems enable adaptive management by continuously analyzing new data and updating recommendations. For example:

• In reforested areas, ML algorithms adjust planting schedules or species selection based on real-time data on soil health and weather conditions.

• Urban NBS projects use ML models to optimize maintenance schedules for green roofs and rain gardens, ensuring sustained performance.

c. Multi-Criteria Decision Analysis

ML models integrate diverse datasets, such as ecological, economic, and social indicators, to support multi-criteria decision-making. For instance:

• When planning green infrastructure in a city, ML systems consider factors like cost, air quality improvement, and public accessibility to identify the most beneficial interventions.

• In rural areas, ML algorithms weigh trade-offs between agricultural productivity and ecosystem conservation to recommend balanced solutions.

4. Applications in Real-World NBS Projects

ML models have been successfully applied in various contexts to optimize resource allocation and assess risks:

a. Urban Heat Island Mitigation

Cities like Singapore and Los Angeles use ML algorithms to prioritize tree planting and green roof installation in areas most affected by heat islands, maximizing cooling effects and energy savings.

b. Coastal Protection

ML models predict erosion patterns and storm surge impacts, guiding the restoration of mangroves and coral reefs to protect vulnerable coastlines in regions like Southeast Asia and the Caribbean.

c. Watershed Management

In projects like the Rhine River restoration, ML systems analyze hydrological and land use data to optimize floodplain reconnection and water quality improvements.

d. Agricultural Landscapes

ML-powered platforms help farmers in Sub-Saharan Africa manage agroforestry systems by optimizing tree planting patterns and irrigation schedules based on real-time environmental data.

5. Challenges and Future Opportunities

Challenges

• **Data Limitations:** ML models require large, high-quality datasets, which may not be available for certain ecosystems or regions.

- **Technical Expertise:** Developing and deploying ML systems requires specialized knowledge, posing a barrier for smaller organizations or communities.

- **Ethical Considerations:** The use of socioeconomic data in ML models must address privacy concerns and avoid reinforcing biases.

Opportunities

- **Integration with IoT and Remote Sensing:** Combining ML with IoT and satellite technologies enhances the accuracy and scalability of models.

- **Open-Source Tools:** Open-source ML platforms democratize access, enabling broader adoption in resource-constrained regions.

- **Collaboration:** Partnerships between governments, NGOs, and technology companies can drive innovation and capacity-building in ML applications for NBS.

Examples of AI Applications in Forest Management, Wetland Restoration, and Urban Green Spaces

AI is revolutionizing the implementation and management of NBS across diverse environments. From managing forests to restoring wetlands and optimizing urban green spaces, AI's ability to analyze complex data and provide actionable insights is transforming how ecosystems are monitored and maintained. This section explores specific examples of AI applications in forest management, wetland restoration, and urban green spaces, showcasing how these technologies contribute to sustainable development and climate resilience.

1. AI in Forest Management

Forests are vital for carbon sequestration, biodiversity conservation, and ecosystem services. AI technologies enhance forest management by improving monitoring, optimizing resource use, and predicting ecosystem responses to environmental changes.

a. Monitoring Forest Health

AI algorithms analyze satellite imagery and data from drones to monitor forest conditions in real time. These tools detect changes in vegetation cover, tree health, and biodiversity:

• **Pest and Disease Detection:** AI systems identify early signs of pests or diseases affecting trees by analyzing patterns in drone imagery and IoT sensor data. For example, AI can detect signs of bark beetle infestations, enabling targeted interventions to prevent widespread damage.

• **Forest Degradation Monitoring:** AI-powered platforms, such as Global Forest Watch, use satellite data to detect illegal logging and deforestation activities. These tools provide actionable insights for conservation agencies to take timely action.

b. Reforestation Planning

AI helps design and implement reforestation projects by selecting optimal tree species and planting locations:

• **Species Selection:** AI models analyze soil quality, climate conditions, and biodiversity requirements to recommend tree species best suited for specific locations. This ensures long-term success and ecological compatibility.

• **Planting Optimization:** AI systems use predictive modeling to design planting patterns that maximize carbon sequestration, reduce erosion, and enhance ecosystem connectivity.

c. Fire Risk Management

AI predicts wildfire risks by analyzing historical fire data, weather patterns, and vegetation conditions:

• **Early Warning Systems:** AI algorithms identify areas at high risk of wildfires, enabling proactive management measures such as creating firebreaks or conducting controlled burns.

• **Post-Fire Recovery:** AI models assess the ecological impact of wildfires and guide reforestation efforts in affected areas.

2. AI in Wetland Restoration

Wetlands play a crucial role in water purification, flood control, and supporting biodiversity. However, these ecosystems are highly sensitive to environmental changes. AI technologies enhance wetland restoration by improving monitoring, guiding interventions, and ensuring long-term sustainability.

a. Water Quality Monitoring

AI systems analyze data from IoT sensors and satellite imagery to monitor water quality in wetlands:

• **Pollution Detection:** AI algorithms detect changes in water chemistry, such as nutrient levels, turbidity, or the presence of harmful algal blooms. For example, AI-powered systems in the Florida Everglades track nutrient loads to guide restoration efforts.

• **Real-Time Insights:** AI processes data from sensors monitoring pH, dissolved oxygen, and temperature, providing real-time updates on wetland health.

b. Flood Mitigation Planning

AI supports the design of wetlands for flood control by simulating hydrological dynamics:

• **Predictive Modeling:** AI models forecast flood events by analyzing rainfall patterns, river flow data, and topography. These predictions help determine the size, location, and configuration of wetlands to maximize floodwater storage capacity.

• **Dynamic Management:** AI tools guide adaptive management by adjusting water levels in restored wetlands based on real-time hydrological data.

c. Habitat Restoration

AI technologies support the restoration of habitats within wetlands, ensuring that they support biodiversity and ecosystem services:

• **Vegetation Mapping:** AI-powered drones create high-resolution maps of wetland vegetation, identifying areas requiring replanting or invasive species removal.

• **Wildlife Monitoring:** AI systems analyze acoustic data to monitor the presence of species, such as frogs or birds, providing indicators of ecosystem health.

3. AI in Urban Green Spaces

Urban green spaces, such as parks, green roofs, and tree-lined streets, enhance urban resilience by reducing heat islands, improving air quality, and promoting well-being. AI technologies optimize the design, management, and impact of these spaces.

a. Urban Heat Island Mitigation

AI models analyze temperature, land use, and vegetation data to mitigate urban heat islands:

• **Cooling Predictions:** AI systems simulate the cooling effects of different interventions, such as tree planting or reflective surfaces, enabling planners to prioritize strategies with the greatest impact.

• **Green Infrastructure Optimization:** AI tools identify locations where green roofs or vertical gardens will provide maximum cooling benefits, particularly in densely populated areas.

b. Air Quality Improvement

AI algorithms monitor air quality in urban areas and guide interventions to reduce pollution:

• **Pollutant Mapping:** AI-powered platforms analyze data from IoT sensors and satellites to map air quality hotspots. These insights inform the placement of trees or green corridors to filter pollutants.

• **Performance Tracking:** AI tracks the effectiveness of urban green spaces in improving air quality over time, ensuring that interventions achieve their intended outcomes.

c. Enhancing Public Accessibility

AI technologies improve the design of urban green spaces to enhance accessibility and equity:

• **Walkability Analysis:** AI models analyze pedestrian movement and public transit data to ensure that green spaces are easily accessible to all communities.

- **Inclusive Design:** AI systems integrate demographic data to recommend features that meet the needs of diverse populations, such as playgrounds, shaded areas, or wheelchair-accessible paths.

4. Challenges and Opportunities in Scaling AI Applications

Challenges

- **Data Availability:** The effectiveness of AI models depends on high-quality data, which may be limited in certain regions or ecosystems.

- **Infrastructure Requirements:** AI technologies require robust computational infrastructure, which may be challenging to implement in resource-constrained areas.

- **Ethical Considerations:** AI applications must address concerns related to data privacy, algorithm bias, and equitable access.

Opportunities

- **Advances in AI Technology:** The development of open-source AI platforms and tools makes these technologies more accessible to NBS practitioners worldwide.

- **Integration with Other Technologies:** Combining AI with IoT, GIS, and remote sensing enhances the accuracy and scalability of NBS monitoring and management systems.

- **Collaborative Approaches:** Partnerships between governments, NGOs, and tech companies can drive innovation and capacity-building in AI applications for NBS.

Chapter 5: Blockchain for Transparency and Collaboration

Blockchain technology is emerging as a powerful tool for enhancing transparency, accountability, and collaboration in NBS. By creating immutable, decentralized digital records, blockchain ensures trust among stakeholders, streamlines project management, and facilitates innovative financing mechanisms. From tracking carbon credits to ensuring equitable resource distribution, blockchain can address key challenges in implementing and scaling NBS.

This chapter explores how blockchain can support NBS by improving transparency in funding and project implementation, fostering stakeholder collaboration, and enabling the verification of ecosystem services. It examines practical applications of blockchain in managing NBS projects and highlights its potential to democratize governance and foster equitable partnerships. Challenges such as accessibility, scalability, and energy use are also discussed, alongside strategies to harness blockchain's potential for advancing sustainable development.

Role of Blockchain in Enhancing Trust and Accountability in Nature-Based Solutions Projects

The successful implementation of NBS often involves a complex network of stakeholders, including governments, private entities, local communities, and non-governmental organizations (NGOs). Ensuring transparency, trust, and accountability among these stakeholders is critical for the success and scalability of NBS projects. Blockchain technology, with its decentralized and immutable nature, has emerged as a transformative tool to address these challenges. By providing a secure and transparent system for tracking transactions, agreements, and outcomes, blockchain enhances trust and accountability in NBS projects, fostering greater collaboration and efficiency.

1. Enhancing Transparency in Funding and Resource Allocation

One of the primary challenges in NBS projects is ensuring that funding and resources are allocated appropriately and transparently. Blockchain offers a robust solution by creating an auditable and tamper-proof digital ledger.

a. Tracking Financial Flows

Blockchain technology allows for real-time tracking of financial transactions, ensuring that funds are used as intended. For instance:

• Donors can trace how their contributions are spent, from the procurement of materials for reforestation to payments for local labor.

• Governments and NGOs can monitor the distribution of resources across multiple NBS sites, ensuring equitable allocation.

b. Reducing Corruption and Mismanagement

The immutable nature of blockchain ensures that all financial transactions are recorded permanently and cannot be altered. This reduces the risk of corruption or mismanagement, particularly in large-scale projects involving multiple intermediaries.

c. Ensuring Accountability in Carbon Markets

In carbon offset projects, blockchain can track the generation and trading of carbon credits with complete transparency. Each credit can be tokenized on the blockchain, providing an unalterable record of its origin, ownership, and use. This builds trust among buyers and sellers, ensuring that the credits genuinely represent environmental benefits.

2. Strengthening Stakeholder Trust

Trust is a cornerstone of successful NBS projects, particularly when diverse stakeholders with varying interests are involved. Blockchain fosters trust by providing a shared, verifiable source of truth.

a. Transparent Agreements

Smart contracts—self-executing agreements encoded on the blockchain—facilitate trust by ensuring that all parties adhere to predefined terms. For example:

• A smart contract in a wetland restoration project could release funds to local contractors only after specific milestones, such as planting vegetation or completing water filtration systems, are verified.

• In reforestation projects, smart contracts can ensure that payments to landowners are contingent on maintaining tree cover for a specified period.

b. Verifiable Ecosystem Outcomes

Blockchain enables the transparent verification of ecosystem outcomes, such as carbon sequestration or biodiversity gains. Data from IoT sensors or satellite imagery can be recorded on the blockchain, providing stakeholders with irrefutable evidence of project performance.

c. Building Community Confidence

Local communities often harbor skepticism about the benefits of NBS projects, particularly when external organizations are involved. Blockchain addresses this by providing communities with access to transparent records of project activities, funding, and outcomes. This inclusivity fosters trust and encourages active participation.

3. Promoting Accountability in Governance

Effective governance is essential for the success of NBS, particularly in large-scale or cross-border projects. Blockchain supports accountable governance by ensuring that all decisions and actions are documented and accessible.

a. Decentralized Decision-Making

Blockchain facilitates decentralized governance, where all stakeholders have an equal say in project decisions. This prevents any single entity from dominating the process and ensures that diverse perspectives are considered.

b. Transparent Voting Mechanisms

Blockchain-based voting systems enable stakeholders to participate in decision-making processes securely and transparently. For instance:

• In watershed management projects, local communities, government agencies, and NGOs can vote on resource allocation or project priorities, with all votes recorded on the blockchain for accountability.

• In urban green infrastructure projects, residents can use blockchain platforms to express preferences for specific interventions, such as tree planting or the creation of public parks.

c. Monitoring Compliance

Blockchain provides an efficient system for monitoring compliance with environmental regulations and project agreements. For example:

• In a mangrove restoration project, blockchain can track whether contractors adhere to guidelines for planting density and species selection.

• In agricultural NBS, blockchain can verify that farmers implement prescribed soil conservation practices to qualify for subsidies or incentives.

4. Enabling Collaborative Partnerships

NBS projects often require collaboration among diverse stakeholders, from policymakers and private investors to researchers and local communities. Blockchain fosters collaboration by providing a shared platform for data sharing and coordination.

a. Data Transparency and Sharing

Blockchain allows stakeholders to share data securely and transparently, reducing information asymmetry and fostering collaboration. For example:

• Researchers can share findings on ecosystem health, such as soil quality or biodiversity levels, with project managers and policymakers in real time.

• Private investors can access transparent records of project performance, increasing their confidence in funding NBS initiatives.

b. Incentivizing Participation

Blockchain-based incentive mechanisms, such as tokenized rewards, encourage stakeholder participation in NBS projects. For instance:

• Community members who contribute to monitoring activities, such as reporting wildlife sightings or maintaining green spaces, can earn digital tokens as rewards.

• Farmers adopting sustainable practices in agricultural NBS projects can receive blockchain-verified payments or credits.

c. Cross-Border Collaboration

For transnational NBS projects, such as river basin restoration or migratory wildlife corridors, blockchain ensures seamless collaboration by providing a unified platform for tracking progress and sharing resources across borders.

5. Challenges and Opportunities

Challenges

• **Technical Complexity:** Blockchain technology requires significant technical expertise for implementation and maintenance, which may be a barrier for smaller organizations.

• **Energy Consumption:** Some blockchain systems, particularly those using proof-of-work mechanisms, are energy-intensive, raising concerns about their environmental impact.

• **Accessibility:** Ensuring that all stakeholders, including local communities, have access to blockchain platforms and understand how to use them is critical for inclusivity.

Opportunities

- **Advancements in Energy-Efficient Blockchains:** Emerging technologies, such as proof-of-stake and other low-energy consensus mechanisms, reduce blockchain's environmental footprint.

- **Integration with IoT and AI:** Combining blockchain with IoT sensors and AI models enhances the accuracy and scalability of monitoring and verification systems.

- **Open-Source Platforms:** The availability of open-source blockchain tools makes it easier for organizations to adopt the technology without incurring high costs.

Applications of Blockchain for Funding, Stakeholder Collaboration, and Verifying Carbon Credits in Nature-Based Solutions

Blockchain technology has the potential to address key challenges in implementing and managing NBS, particularly in the areas of funding, stakeholder collaboration, and verifying carbon credits. By leveraging its decentralized, transparent, and immutable characteristics, blockchain ensures that resources are managed efficiently, stakeholders are aligned in their goals, and carbon offset mechanisms are credible and trustworthy. This section explores how blockchain can be applied in these areas to enhance the effectiveness and scalability of NBS projects.

1. Enhancing Funding Mechanisms for NBS

Securing and managing funding is a critical component of successful NBS projects. Blockchain technology offers innovative solutions to streamline funding processes, increase transparency, and ensure accountability in resource utilization.

a. Crowdfunding for NBS Projects

Blockchain-based crowdfunding platforms allow individuals and organizations to contribute directly to NBS projects. These platforms:

• Use smart contracts to ensure that funds are released only when specific milestones are achieved, increasing donor confidence.

• Provide real-time visibility into how contributions are being used, fostering transparency and trust.

For example, a blockchain-enabled platform for reforestation could allow donors to track their contributions from planting to the growth of trees, ensuring that their funds have a tangible impact.

b. Tokenization of Environmental Assets

Blockchain enables the tokenization of environmental assets, such as forest areas or restored wetlands, which can be bought and sold as digital tokens. These tokens:

• Represent a share in the environmental benefits of an NBS project, such as carbon sequestration or biodiversity enhancement.

• Attract investors by providing a tradeable asset, thereby mobilizing private sector funding for NBS.

c. Transparent Grant Management

Blockchain can improve the management of grants for NBS by creating a digital ledger of transactions. For instance:

• Government agencies and NGOs can use blockchain to monitor how grant funds are distributed and utilized.

• Funders can trace their contributions to specific activities, such as wetland restoration or the creation of urban green spaces.

2. Strengthening Stakeholder Collaboration

NBS projects often involve multiple stakeholders, including governments, private investors, local communities, and NGOs. Blockchain facilitates collaboration by providing a shared, transparent platform for communication, decision-making, and data sharing.

a. Shared Data Platforms

Blockchain creates a unified platform where stakeholders can share data securely and transparently. For example:

• Researchers can upload findings on ecosystem health, such as water quality or biodiversity metrics, allowing all stakeholders to access and use this information.

• Communities can contribute data, such as local observations or maintenance reports, ensuring that their knowledge is integrated into decision-making.

b. Smart Contracts for Collaborative Agreements

Smart contracts are self-executing agreements encoded on the blockchain that automatically enforce terms when specific conditions are met. These contracts:

• Ensure accountability among stakeholders by automating payments, resource distribution, or project milestones.

• Simplify complex arrangements, such as those involving multiple funding sources or cross-border collaborations.

For instance, in a wetland restoration project, a smart contract could release payments to contractors only after sensors verify that specific water quality targets have been met.

c. Inclusive Participation

Blockchain promotes inclusivity by giving all stakeholders access to the same information and decision-making tools. For example:

• Local communities can participate in project governance through blockchain-based voting systems, ensuring that their voices are heard.

• Small-scale farmers or landowners can engage with private investors transparently, fostering equitable partnerships.

3. Verifying Carbon Credits

Carbon credits are an essential tool for funding NBS, but their credibility and traceability are often questioned. Blockchain addresses these issues by creating a transparent, tamper-proof system for tracking the generation, ownership, and use of carbon credits.

a. Transparent Carbon Credit Lifecycle

Blockchain provides a complete, auditable record of a carbon credit's lifecycle, from its creation to its retirement. For instance:

• In a mangrove restoration project, blockchain records every stage, from the initial planting to the quantification of carbon sequestration.

• Buyers of carbon credits can verify their authenticity and origin, ensuring that they represent genuine environmental benefits.

b. Preventing Double Counting

One of the challenges in carbon markets is the double counting of credits, where the same carbon reduction is claimed by multiple entities. Blockchain eliminates this issue by:

• Creating a unique digital identity for each carbon credit, ensuring that it can only be claimed once.

• Providing a transparent system for tracking ownership and transactions.

c. Enabling Smaller-Scale Participation

Blockchain lowers the barriers to entry for smaller-scale carbon credit producers, such as smallholder farmers or community-led reforestation projects. These producers can:

• Tokenize their carbon credits and sell them directly to buyers, bypassing intermediaries and retaining a larger share of the revenue.

• Use blockchain to demonstrate the credibility of their efforts, attracting more buyers.

d. Integrating IoT for Verification

Blockchain can integrate data from IoT sensors and remote sensing technologies to verify the environmental impact of NBS. For example:

• IoT sensors in reforested areas track tree growth and carbon absorption, feeding this data into the blockchain.

• Satellite imagery verifies land use changes, such as the establishment of wetlands, ensuring that reported carbon reductions are accurate.

4. Challenges and Opportunities

Challenges

• **Technical Complexity:** Implementing blockchain systems requires technical expertise, which may not be available in all regions.

• **Cost Barriers:** The setup and maintenance of blockchain platforms can be expensive, particularly for small-scale NBS projects.

• **Scalability:** Blockchain systems must handle large volumes of data efficiently to support extensive NBS networks.

Opportunities

• **Integration with Other Technologies:** Combining blockchain with AI, IoT, and GIS enhances its capabilities for NBS monitoring and management.

• **Energy-Efficient Blockchains:** Emerging blockchain protocols, such as proof-of-stake, reduce energy consumption, addressing environmental concerns.

• **Collaborative Models:** Governments, NGOs, and private sector entities can work together to develop blockchain solutions tailored to NBS.

Blockchain's Potential for Fostering Decentralized and Equitable NBS Governance

Governance plays a critical role in the success of NBS, particularly in projects involving diverse stakeholders and spanning multiple geographic regions. Effective governance ensures transparent decision-making, equitable resource distribution, and long-term sustainability. Blockchain technology, with its decentralized, transparent, and secure infrastructure, has the potential to revolutionize NBS governance by addressing inefficiencies, promoting inclusivity, and enabling collaboration among stakeholders. This section explores how blockchain fosters decentralized and equitable governance, ensuring that NBS projects achieve their intended environmental and societal benefits.

1. Decentralized Decision-Making in NBS Projects

Traditional governance models often rely on hierarchical structures, which can lead to inefficiencies, exclusion of key stakeholders, and lack of accountability. Blockchain offers a decentralized approach, enabling all stakeholders to participate in decision-making processes.

a. Blockchain as a Decentralized Ledger

Blockchain's distributed ledger technology ensures that all stakeholders have access to the same, up-to-date information. This transparency:

• Reduces power imbalances by preventing any single entity from controlling or altering project data.

• Encourages collaborative decision-making, as all participants can view and verify transactions, milestones, and outcomes.

For instance, in a watershed management project, blockchain could provide a transparent record of water usage, enabling upstream and downstream communities to collaborate on equitable resource distribution.

b. Smart Contracts for Automated Governance

Smart contracts—self-executing agreements encoded on the blockchain—facilitate decentralized governance by automating processes based on predefined conditions. For example:

• In a reforestation project, a smart contract could ensure that payments to contractors are released only after satellite data verifies that a specific area has been successfully reforested.

• In urban green infrastructure projects, smart contracts can automatically allocate maintenance budgets based on data from IoT sensors monitoring the health of green roofs or urban parks.

c. Participatory Decision-Making Platforms

Blockchain-based platforms allow stakeholders to vote on key decisions, such as resource allocation or project priorities. These platforms:

• Ensure that all votes are securely recorded and cannot be tampered with, fostering trust in the decision-making process.

• Enable broader participation, particularly from marginalized groups, by providing a secure and accessible digital space for engagement.

For example, residents of a city implementing green infrastructure could use a blockchain-based platform to vote on the placement of new parks or tree-planting initiatives.

2. Promoting Equity Through Transparent Resource Distribution

Equitable governance is essential to ensure that the benefits of NBS are shared fairly among all stakeholders, particularly vulnerable and marginalized communities. Blockchain enhances equity by providing transparency and accountability in resource distribution.

a. Transparent Allocation of Funds

Blockchain creates an immutable record of financial transactions, ensuring that funds are distributed as intended. For example:

• In a coastal restoration project, blockchain could track funding from donors to local contractors and suppliers, ensuring that all parties are compensated fairly.

• Governments and NGOs can use blockchain to monitor grant distributions, preventing mismanagement or corruption.

b. Empowering Local Communities

Blockchain allows local communities to participate actively in governance and receive direct benefits from NBS projects. For instance:

• Smallholder farmers adopting sustainable practices in an agroforestry project could receive blockchain-verified payments or carbon credits, ensuring transparency and fairness.

• Community members contributing to the maintenance of urban green spaces could earn tokenized rewards, encouraging participation and stewardship.

c. Addressing Power Imbalances

In traditional governance models, powerful stakeholders often dominate decision-making, marginalizing smaller entities or local communities. Blockchain's decentralized nature levels the playing field by:

• Providing equal access to information for all participants, regardless of their size or influence.

• Creating accountability mechanisms, such as publicly verifiable records of decisions and actions, to prevent abuse of power.

3. Enhancing Accountability in Cross-Border NBS Governance

Many NBS projects, such as river basin restoration or migratory wildlife corridors, span national borders and involve multiple jurisdictions. Blockchain addresses the governance challenges in such projects by providing a unified, transparent platform for collaboration.

a. Unified Governance Frameworks

Blockchain enables the creation of cross-border governance frameworks, ensuring that all stakeholders operate under the same rules and conditions. For example:

• In a transboundary river basin project, blockchain could track water usage, pollution levels, and restoration efforts across countries, providing a shared source of truth for all parties.

• Migratory species conservation projects could use blockchain to monitor habitat conditions and coordinate protection efforts across regions.

b. Real-Time Data Sharing

Blockchain facilitates real-time data sharing among stakeholders, improving coordination and decision-making. For instance:

• Governments, NGOs, and local communities involved in a wetland restoration project could use blockchain to share data on water quality, vegetation health, and biodiversity metrics.

• Private sector partners in an urban green infrastructure initiative could access blockchain-verified performance data to evaluate the impact of their investments.

c. Enforcing Compliance

Blockchain's transparency ensures that all stakeholders are held accountable for their commitments. For example:

• A blockchain-based system could monitor compliance with environmental regulations, such as limits on deforestation or water pollution, in a large-scale reforestation project.

• Smart contracts could automatically impose penalties or adjust resource allocations if stakeholders fail to meet agreed-upon targets.

4. Challenges and Opportunities

Challenges

• **Technical Barriers:** Implementing blockchain requires technical expertise and robust infrastructure, which may not be available in all regions.

• **Digital Divide:** Ensuring that marginalized communities have access to blockchain platforms and understand how to use them is critical for equitable governance.

• **Scalability:** Managing large datasets and numerous transactions on a blockchain can be resource-intensive, particularly for large-scale NBS projects.

Opportunities

• **Energy-Efficient Blockchain Solutions:** Emerging technologies, such as proof-of-stake mechanisms, reduce the environmental impact of blockchain systems.

• **Integration with IoT and Remote Sensing:** Combining blockchain with other digital tools enhances its capabilities for monitoring and verifying NBS outcomes.

• **Collaborative Models:** Partnerships between governments, NGOs, private companies, and tech developers can address technical and resource challenges, enabling broader adoption of blockchain for NBS governance.

Chapter 6: Digital Twin Technology for Nature-Based Solutions Planning and Simulation

Digital Twin Technology is revolutionizing the planning and implementation of NBS by creating virtual replicas of ecosystems and infrastructure. These digital models simulate real-world conditions, enabling stakeholders to test various scenarios, optimize designs, and predict outcomes before actual implementation. By integrating real-time data and advanced analytics, digital twins enhance decision-making, reduce risks, and improve the efficiency and effectiveness of NBS projects.

This chapter delves into the role of digital twin technology in NBS, exploring its applications in planning, simulating interventions, and visualizing ecosystem dynamics. It highlights the advantages of using digital twins for designing resilient, adaptive, and scalable solutions, while also addressing challenges such as data requirements, accessibility, and technological complexity. Through digital twin technology, NBS can achieve greater precision and impact in addressing climate resilience and sustainability challenges.

Introduction to Digital Twins and Their Relevance to Nature-Based Solutions

Digital Twin Technology is rapidly emerging as a game-changing innovation in the design and management of complex systems, including NBS. A digital twin is a virtual replica of a physical entity, such as an ecosystem, infrastructure, or an entire landscape, that is continuously updated with real-time data. By mirroring the behavior, conditions, and performance of real-world systems, digital twins allow stakeholders to simulate scenarios, optimize designs, and predict outcomes with unprecedented accuracy. This technology holds immense potential for enhancing the planning, implementation, and long-term success of NBS projects.

1. What Are Digital Twins?

Digital twins are dynamic digital models that integrate data from sensors, IoT devices, and other sources to replicate the physical world. Unlike static models or simulations, digital twins are interactive and constantly updated, providing a real-time representation of their physical counterparts.

a. Components of a Digital Twin

• **Physical Entity:** The real-world system being mirrored, such as a wetland, forest, or urban green space.

• **Digital Model:** The virtual representation of the physical entity, created using advanced software and data analytics tools.

• **Data Integration:** Continuous data flows from IoT sensors, drones, remote sensing, and other monitoring technologies, ensuring the digital twin reflects real-time conditions.

• **Analytics and Feedback:** Advanced algorithms analyze the data, generate insights, and provide actionable feedback for decision-making.

b. Key Features of Digital Twins

• **Real-Time Monitoring:** Digital twins provide live updates on the condition and performance of NBS, enabling dynamic management.

• **Predictive Capabilities:** By simulating various scenarios, digital twins predict how ecosystems will respond to changes, such as climate variations or human interventions.

• **Interactive Visualization:** Users can explore and manipulate digital twins through intuitive interfaces, gaining a deeper understanding of complex systems.

2. The Relevance of Digital Twins to NBS

NBS are inherently complex, involving dynamic interactions between natural systems, human activities, and external factors such as climate change. Digital twins provide a powerful tool for managing this complexity, enabling stakeholders to plan, implement, and adapt NBS more effectively.

a. Addressing Complexity in Ecosystems

Ecosystems are characterized by interdependent processes that can be challenging to understand and predict. Digital twins allow stakeholders to model these processes with precision, providing insights into:

• Water flow dynamics in wetlands and watersheds.

• Carbon sequestration potential of reforestation projects.

• Biodiversity patterns in urban green spaces and natural reserves.

By capturing these dynamics in a digital twin, stakeholders can anticipate challenges and design solutions that align with ecosystem behavior.

b. Supporting Climate Resilience

Digital twins play a critical role in designing NBS that enhance resilience to climate change. For example:

• In coastal areas, digital twins simulate the impact of sea level rise and storm surges on mangroves and other protective ecosystems, guiding restoration efforts.

• In urban settings, they model the cooling effects of green roofs and tree canopies under different temperature scenarios, optimizing interventions to combat heat islands.

c. Enhancing Stakeholder Collaboration

Digital twins serve as a shared platform for collaboration among diverse stakeholders, including governments, NGOs, private companies, and local communities. By visualizing NBS projects in a digital environment, stakeholders can:

• Align on goals and priorities through a common understanding of project dynamics.

• Explore trade-offs and synergies, such as balancing flood mitigation with biodiversity conservation.

• Engage communities by demonstrating the tangible benefits of proposed interventions.

3. Applications of Digital Twins in NBS

The relevance of digital twins extends across various stages of NBS planning and management, offering practical applications that improve outcomes and efficiency.

a. Planning and Design

During the planning phase, digital twins enable stakeholders to test different designs and configurations, ensuring that NBS align with ecological and societal objectives. For example:

• In reforestation projects, digital twins predict how different tree species and planting densities will impact soil health, carbon sequestration, and biodiversity.

• In watershed management, they model the effects of riparian buffers on water quality and flow patterns, optimizing placement and scale.

b. Real-Time Monitoring

Digital twins provide continuous monitoring of NBS, allowing managers to track performance and respond to emerging issues. For example:

• In constructed wetlands, digital twins monitor water quality metrics, such as nutrient levels and turbidity, identifying maintenance needs in real time.

• In urban green spaces, they track vegetation health and air quality improvements, ensuring interventions meet their targets.

c. Adaptive Management

The predictive capabilities of digital twins support adaptive management by simulating the outcomes of different strategies. For example:

• In agroforestry systems, digital twins predict how changes in planting schedules or irrigation practices will affect crop yields and ecosystem services.

• In coastal restoration, they model the impact of removing invasive species on native biodiversity and shoreline stability.

4. Benefits of Digital Twins for NBS

Digital twins offer several advantages that make them an invaluable tool for advancing NBS:

a. Improved Decision-Making

By providing accurate and comprehensive data, digital twins enable stakeholders to make informed decisions that maximize the benefits of NBS.

b. Risk Reduction

Simulating scenarios in a digital environment reduces the risks associated with implementing NBS. For example, digital twins can test flood mitigation designs before physical construction begins, minimizing potential failures.

c. Cost Efficiency

Although developing a digital twin involves upfront investment, it reduces long-term costs by improving resource allocation and preventing costly errors.

d. Scalability

Digital twins support the scalability of NBS by providing a replicable framework for planning and monitoring projects across different contexts and geographies.

5. Challenges and Future Directions

While digital twins hold immense potential, their application in NBS is not without challenges:

Challenges

• **Data Requirements:** Developing a digital twin requires extensive data, which may not be available for all ecosystems.

• **Technical Expertise:** Creating and managing digital twins demands specialized skills, posing a barrier for some organizations.

• **Cost and Infrastructure:** The technology can be resource-intensive, particularly for small-scale projects or resource-constrained regions.

Future Directions

• **Integration with AI and IoT:** Combining digital twins with AI algorithms and IoT sensors enhances their capabilities, enabling more accurate simulations and real-time updates.

• **Open-Source Platforms:** Developing open-source tools can make digital twin technology more accessible to smaller organizations and developing countries.

• **Community Engagement:** Leveraging digital twins as an educational and participatory tool can enhance public support for NBS and foster collaborative decision-making.

Applications in Simulating and Testing Various NBS Interventions Before Implementation

NBS are complex, involving dynamic interactions between natural systems and human activities. Implementing NBS without adequate testing can lead to suboptimal results, inefficiencies, and unintended consequences. Digital twin technology offers a transformative approach to address these challenges by creating virtual replicas of ecosystems or interventions. These digital models simulate real-world conditions, allowing stakeholders to test various NBS interventions in a risk-free environment before committing to physical implementation. This approach ensures that resources are used efficiently, outcomes are optimized, and potential risks are mitigated.

1. Simulating Hydrological Dynamics for Water Management

Hydrological dynamics, such as water flow, storage, and quality, are critical components of many NBS projects. Digital twins simulate these processes to optimize interventions in wetlands, rivers, and floodplains.

a. Wetland Restoration and Flood Mitigation

Digital twins of wetlands simulate how interventions will impact water retention, filtration, and flood regulation:

• **Flood Management:** In flood-prone areas, digital twins model water flow during extreme rainfall events, testing the effectiveness of restored wetlands or floodplains in mitigating flood risks. These simulations help determine the optimal size, location, and configuration of wetlands to maximize floodwater storage capacity.

• **Water Quality Improvements:** By modeling nutrient and sediment dynamics, digital twins assess the potential of wetlands to filter pollutants from agricultural runoff, guiding the design of interventions to enhance water quality.

b. Urban Stormwater Management

Digital twins simulate stormwater flow in urban areas, enabling planners to test green infrastructure solutions such as rain gardens, bioswales, and green roofs:

• **Scenario Testing:** Planners can evaluate how different green infrastructure configurations will reduce runoff, prevent flooding, and improve water infiltration.

• **Optimizing Placement:** Simulations identify the most effective locations for stormwater interventions, ensuring that limited resources are used efficiently.

2. Optimizing Forest and Vegetation-Based Solutions

Forests, urban green spaces, and other vegetation-based solutions play a critical role in climate mitigation, biodiversity conservation, and ecosystem restoration. Digital twins allow stakeholders to test and refine these interventions.

a. Reforestation and Afforestation

Digital twins simulate tree planting strategies to maximize carbon sequestration, soil stabilization, and habitat connectivity:

• **Species Selection:** By integrating data on soil quality, climate conditions, and biodiversity needs, digital twins recommend the most suitable tree species for specific locations.

• **Planting Density:** Simulations test different planting densities to optimize growth rates, carbon storage, and ecological benefits.

b. Urban Green Infrastructure

Digital twins model the impact of urban vegetation on air quality, temperature regulation, and human well-being:

• **Cooling Effects:** Simulations predict how tree canopies, green walls, and green roofs reduce urban heat islands under various climate scenarios. This helps prioritize interventions in areas most affected by extreme heat.

• **Air Pollution Reduction:** By analyzing pollutant dispersion patterns, digital twins determine the best locations for vegetation to filter pollutants and improve air quality.

c. Agroforestry Systems

In agricultural landscapes, digital twins test agroforestry designs to balance productivity with environmental benefits:

• **Erosion Control:** Simulations evaluate how tree rows, hedgerows, or buffer strips reduce soil erosion on slopes.

• **Crop Yield Optimization:** Digital twins assess the impact of tree placement on microclimates and soil health, guiding the integration of agroforestry into existing farming systems.

3. Designing Coastal and Marine NBS

Coastal and marine ecosystems are vital for protecting shorelines, supporting biodiversity, and providing livelihoods. Digital twins simulate interventions in these environments to ensure their resilience and effectiveness.

a. Mangrove Restoration

Mangroves act as natural barriers against storm surges and coastal erosion. Digital twins model the restoration of mangroves to optimize their protective functions:

• **Tidal Flow Modeling:** Simulations predict how tidal patterns will interact with restored mangroves, ensuring that planting locations and densities maximize erosion control and storm surge mitigation.

• **Sediment Dynamics:** Digital twins analyze sediment deposition and erosion, guiding strategies to stabilize shorelines and enhance mangrove growth.

b. Coral Reef Restoration

Coral reefs protect coastlines from wave energy while supporting marine biodiversity. Digital twins simulate reef restoration projects to improve their success:

• **Wave Energy Reduction:** Simulations assess how artificial or restored reefs attenuate wave energy under different storm scenarios, helping design reefs that provide maximum coastal protection.

• **Biodiversity Enhancement:** By modeling habitat conditions, digital twins predict which reef designs will support the greatest diversity of marine species.

c. Living Shorelines

Living shorelines combine natural and engineered elements to stabilize coastlines. Digital twins test different designs to balance ecological and protective functions:

• **Material Selection:** Simulations evaluate the performance of materials like oyster shells, vegetation, and natural fiber mats in stabilizing shorelines.

• **Scalability Testing:** Digital twins assess how living shorelines perform at different scales, from small community projects to large coastal defense systems.

4. Testing Biodiversity and Ecosystem Connectivity

Biodiversity and ecosystem connectivity are core objectives of many NBS projects. Digital twins simulate the interactions between species, habitats, and human activities to guide conservation efforts.

a. Wildlife Corridors

Digital twins model the design of wildlife corridors to ensure connectivity between fragmented habitats:

• **Species Movement Simulation:** By analyzing data on animal behavior and habitat preferences, digital twins predict how species will use corridors, optimizing their placement and design.

• **Barrier Identification:** Simulations identify potential barriers, such as roads or urban areas, and test solutions like overpasses or underpasses to facilitate safe movement.

b. Habitat Restoration

Restoring degraded habitats requires careful planning to ensure ecological balance. Digital twins simulate restoration efforts to predict their impact on biodiversity:

• **Vegetation Dynamics:** Simulations model how plant species will interact and compete in restored areas, helping select combinations that maximize biodiversity.

• **Climate Adaptation:** Digital twins predict how restored habitats will respond to changing climate conditions, guiding adaptive strategies for long-term resilience.

5. Benefits of Simulating NBS Interventions

Simulating NBS interventions using digital twins offers numerous advantages:

a. Risk Reduction

By testing interventions in a virtual environment, stakeholders can identify and address potential challenges before physical implementation, minimizing risks and ensuring project success.

b. Cost Efficiency

Simulations reduce the need for costly trial-and-error approaches, optimizing resource allocation and minimizing waste.

c. Improved Design

Digital twins enable iterative testing and refinement, ensuring that interventions are tailored to local conditions and objectives.

d. Stakeholder Engagement

Interactive simulations help communicate the benefits of NBS to stakeholders, fostering collaboration and support for projects.

Benefits of Visualizing Ecosystem Services and Predicting Future Scenarios with Digital Twins

Digital twin technology offers transformative capabilities for visualizing ecosystem services and predicting future scenarios in the context of NBS. By creating virtual replicas of ecosystems that integrate real-time and historical data, digital twins allow stakeholders to understand complex ecological processes, forecast potential outcomes, and optimize interventions. These benefits are critical for ensuring the success and scalability of NBS, enabling decision-makers to maximize ecosystem benefits while minimizing risks.

1. Visualizing Ecosystem Services

Ecosystem services, such as water filtration, carbon sequestration, biodiversity support, and flood regulation, are often difficult to measure and communicate effectively. Digital twins provide a dynamic platform for visualizing these services, making them more tangible and accessible to stakeholders.

a. Quantifying Ecosystem Benefits

Digital twins enable precise quantification of ecosystem services by integrating data from sensors, satellite imagery, and field observations. For example:

• **Carbon Sequestration:** Digital twins simulate carbon absorption by forests, wetlands, or grasslands, providing real-time metrics on carbon storage and flux.

• **Water Filtration:** In wetlands or riparian zones, digital twins visualize how vegetation and soil filter pollutants from water, helping stakeholders understand the benefits of these interventions.

• **Biodiversity Metrics:** By analyzing habitat connectivity and species data, digital twins offer insights into the biodiversity benefits of reforestation, green corridors, or marine reserves.

b. Interactive Visualization

The ability to interact with digital twins through user-friendly interfaces enhances stakeholder understanding and engagement. For example:

• Policymakers can explore the effects of different interventions on flood regulation, water quality, or air purification.

• Communities can visualize how proposed NBS projects, such as urban parks or coastal restoration, will enhance local ecosystem services and quality of life.

c. Communicating Value to Stakeholders

Visualizing ecosystem services helps bridge the gap between scientific data and public understanding:

• Private investors can see the tangible return on investment for funding NBS projects, such as increased carbon offsets or reduced flood damages.

• Local communities can better appreciate the environmental and social benefits of proposed interventions, fostering support and participation.

2. Predicting Future Scenarios

Digital twins go beyond static visualization by simulating future scenarios, enabling stakeholders to anticipate challenges and plan adaptive strategies. This predictive capability is particularly valuable in the face of climate change, urbanization, and other dynamic pressures on ecosystems.

a. Climate Change Adaptation

Digital twins model the impacts of climate change on ecosystems, helping stakeholders design resilient NBS interventions:

• **Rising Temperatures:** Simulations predict how urban green spaces, such as parks or green roofs, mitigate urban heat islands under different temperature scenarios.

• **Sea Level Rise:** In coastal areas, digital twins forecast the effects of rising seas on mangroves, coral reefs, or living shorelines, guiding restoration efforts to maximize protection.

• **Drought and Water Scarcity:** Digital twins analyze water availability in agricultural or forested landscapes, supporting strategies for drought-tolerant vegetation or water-efficient irrigation.

b. Extreme Weather Events

Predicting the impact of extreme weather events, such as storms, floods, or wildfires, is critical for ensuring the success of NBS:

• **Flood Scenarios:** Digital twins simulate river flow and stormwater runoff during heavy rainfall, testing the effectiveness of wetlands or floodplains in mitigating floods.

• **Storm Surges:** In coastal environments, digital twins model the protective effects of mangroves or dunes against storm surges, helping planners optimize these natural defenses.

• **Wildfire Risk:** By analyzing vegetation, soil moisture, and weather data, digital twins predict wildfire risks and guide preventative measures, such as controlled burns or vegetation management.

c. Urban Development and Land Use Changes

Urbanization and land use changes can have significant impacts on ecosystems. Digital twins help stakeholders explore how these changes affect NBS and ecosystem services:

• **Urban Expansion:** Simulations predict the effects of urban growth on air quality, water resources, and green space availability, guiding sustainable urban planning.

• **Agricultural Land Use:** In rural areas, digital twins model the trade-offs between agricultural productivity and ecosystem conservation, supporting balanced land use decisions.

3. Supporting Adaptive Management

The ability to visualize ecosystem services and predict future scenarios supports adaptive management, ensuring that NBS remain effective under changing conditions.

a. Scenario Testing

Digital twins allow stakeholders to test multiple scenarios and compare outcomes, helping them select the most effective strategies:

• In reforestation projects, stakeholders can simulate different tree species, planting densities, or irrigation schedules to optimize carbon sequestration and biodiversity.

• In urban green infrastructure projects, planners can test various configurations of parks, green roofs, or rain gardens to maximize cooling and stormwater management.

b. Real-Time Monitoring and Feedback

By integrating real-time data, digital twins provide continuous feedback on the performance of NBS:

• IoT sensors in wetlands or forests feed data into the digital twin, enabling stakeholders to track progress and adjust management practices as needed.

• In urban areas, air quality or temperature sensors provide real-time insights into the benefits of green infrastructure, supporting timely interventions.

c. Proactive Risk Management

Predictive simulations enable stakeholders to anticipate and mitigate risks before they materialize:

• For example, digital twins can identify vulnerabilities in coastal defenses, such as eroding dunes or degraded mangroves, prompting early restoration efforts.

• In watersheds, simulations highlight areas at risk of nutrient runoff or sedimentation, guiding preventative measures like riparian buffers or contour farming.

4. Advantages of Digital Twins in NBS

a. Increased Efficiency

Digital twins optimize resource allocation by identifying the most effective interventions and minimizing trial-and-error approaches.

b. Enhanced Collaboration

Interactive visualization and scenario testing foster collaboration among diverse stakeholders, ensuring that decisions are informed by a shared understanding of ecosystem dynamics.

c. Long-Term Sustainability

By predicting future scenarios, digital twins help stakeholders design NBS that remain effective and sustainable over time, even as conditions change.

d. Broader Support

The ability to communicate the tangible benefits of NBS through digital twins enhances public and private sector support, mobilizing resources and participation.

Chapter 7: Data-Driven Decision-Making and Governance

In the planning, implementation, and management of NBS, data-driven approaches have become essential for informed decision-making and effective governance. High-quality data enables stakeholders to understand complex ecological systems, monitor interventions, and adapt to changing conditions, ensuring that NBS deliver long-term benefits. Governance frameworks rooted in data transparency and accessibility foster collaboration, accountability, and equity among diverse stakeholders.

This chapter explores the role of data in shaping NBS projects, from collecting and analyzing environmental metrics to informing collaborative governance models. It highlights digital platforms as tools for sharing insights, engaging stakeholders, and ensuring accountability in decision-making processes. The chapter also addresses the ethical considerations and challenges associated with data use, emphasizing the importance of inclusivity and trust in leveraging data for sustainable and resilient NBS governance.

The Importance of High-Quality Data in Designing and Implementing Nature-Based Solutions

High-quality data serves as the foundation for the successful design, implementation, and management of NBS. By providing accurate, reliable, and comprehensive information about environmental conditions and ecosystem dynamics, data enables decision-makers to create effective, efficient, and sustainable interventions. In an era where climate change and environmental degradation demand innovative solutions, leveraging high-quality data ensures that NBS achieve their intended outcomes and adapt to changing circumstances.

1. Enabling Evidence-Based Decision-Making

The complexity of ecosystems and the dynamic nature of environmental challenges make evidence-based decision-making essential for NBS. High-quality data provides the scientific foundation for designing interventions that address specific environmental and social needs.

a. Understanding Ecosystem Dynamics

Ecosystems are governed by intricate relationships between biotic and abiotic components, including vegetation, soil, water, and climate. High-quality data captures these interactions, allowing stakeholders to:

• Analyze ecosystem health, such as biodiversity levels, carbon storage, and nutrient cycles.

• Identify areas of degradation or vulnerability, such as eroded soils or deforested landscapes.

• Predict how ecosystems will respond to interventions, ensuring that NBS are tailored to local conditions.

For example, in a wetland restoration project, data on water flow patterns, sediment dynamics, and vegetation types helps design interventions that optimize water retention and filtration.

b. Defining Objectives and Indicators

Data is critical for setting measurable objectives and defining key performance indicators (KPIs) for NBS. For instance:

• A reforestation project may aim to sequester a specific amount of carbon over a defined period, requiring baseline data on soil carbon content and tree growth rates.

• An urban green infrastructure project may target reductions in air pollution or urban heat, guided by data on current pollution levels and temperature hotspots.

By establishing clear goals and metrics, high-quality data ensures that NBS are designed with measurable and achievable outcomes.

2. Optimizing Resource Allocation

NBS often require significant investments of time, labor, and financial resources. High-quality data ensures that these resources are allocated efficiently, maximizing the impact of interventions.

a. Identifying Priority Areas

Data-driven mapping and analysis help identify areas where NBS will have the greatest environmental and social benefits. For example:

• Remote sensing data can highlight regions most vulnerable to flooding, guiding the placement of floodplain restoration projects.

• Biodiversity surveys can identify habitats in need of conservation, informing the design of wildlife corridors or protected areas.

b. Avoiding Unintended Consequences

High-quality data minimizes the risk of unintended consequences by providing insights into potential trade-offs and synergies. For instance:

• Data on water availability ensures that agroforestry projects do not exacerbate local water scarcity.

• Climate models help predict how reforestation efforts will affect local weather patterns, avoiding adverse impacts on nearby agricultural systems.

c. Supporting Cost-Effective Solutions

By identifying the most impactful interventions, data helps stakeholders allocate resources where they are needed most. For example:

• Hydrological data guides the design of wetlands that provide maximum flood mitigation with minimal construction costs.

• Air quality data informs the placement of urban trees to optimize pollution reduction.

3. Enhancing Monitoring and Evaluation

The success of NBS depends on continuous monitoring and adaptive management. High-quality data is essential for tracking progress, evaluating effectiveness, and making necessary adjustments.

a. Establishing Baselines

Baseline data provides a reference point for measuring the impact of NBS interventions. For example:

• In a reforestation project, baseline data on soil quality and carbon content allows for accurate assessment of improvements over time.

• In urban green infrastructure, initial air quality and temperature data provide benchmarks for evaluating the cooling and pollution-reducing effects of interventions.

b. Real-Time Monitoring

Technologies such as IoT sensors, drones, and satellite imagery generate real-time data that informs adaptive management. For example:

• Water quality sensors in wetlands detect changes in nutrient levels, prompting timely maintenance to prevent eutrophication.

• Temperature sensors in urban green spaces monitor cooling effects during heatwaves, guiding adjustments to vegetation density or irrigation schedules.

c. Long-Term Impact Assessment

High-quality data supports the long-term evaluation of NBS, ensuring that interventions remain effective and resilient. For instance:

• Biodiversity surveys track species recovery in restored habitats, providing insights into ecosystem health.

• Climate models analyze the cumulative carbon sequestration benefits of afforestation projects, demonstrating their contribution to global mitigation goals.

4. Building Stakeholder Trust and Collaboration

Data transparency and accessibility are crucial for fostering trust and collaboration among stakeholders in NBS projects. High-quality data ensures that decisions are evidence-based and accountable, encouraging participation and support.

a. Engaging Local Communities

Local communities often play a critical role in the success of NBS. High-quality data:

124

• Provides clear evidence of the benefits of interventions, such as improved water quality or reduced flood risks, fostering community buy-in.

• Incorporates community observations and knowledge, enhancing the accuracy and relevance of data.

b. Attracting Funding and Investment

Private investors, governments, and NGOs are more likely to support NBS projects backed by robust data. For example:

• Carbon credit markets rely on high-quality data to verify the sequestration benefits of reforestation projects.

• Donors expect transparent reporting on the outcomes of funded interventions, enabled by reliable monitoring data.

c. Facilitating Cross-Sector Collaboration

Data serves as a common language for diverse stakeholders, including scientists, policymakers, and practitioners. By providing a shared understanding of challenges and opportunities, high-quality data enhances collaboration and coordination.

5. Overcoming Challenges in Data Collection and Use

While the benefits of high-quality data are clear, challenges in data collection and use must be addressed to maximize its potential in NBS.

a. Data Gaps and Accessibility

In some regions, particularly in developing countries, data on ecosystems and environmental conditions may be scarce or outdated.

Investments in data collection technologies, such as satellite monitoring and IoT sensors, are critical to bridging these gaps.

b. Data Integration

NBS projects often involve multiple data sources, including remote sensing, field surveys, and community observations. Integrating these datasets into a cohesive framework ensures that decisions are informed by comprehensive and accurate information.

c. Ethical Considerations

The collection and use of data must respect ethical principles, such as privacy and inclusivity. For example:

• Community engagement should involve transparent communication about how data will be used and who will have access to it.

• Efforts should be made to ensure that marginalized groups are not excluded from data-driven decision-making processes.

Digital Platforms for Collaborative Governance and Stakeholder Engagement in Nature-Based Solutions

Effective governance and stakeholder engagement are vital for the success of NBS. Given the complexity of ecosystems and the diverse stakeholders involved in implementing and managing NBS projects, traditional governance models often fall short in addressing dynamic environmental challenges. Digital platforms offer innovative tools for fostering collaboration, improving decision-making, and ensuring accountability among stakeholders. By providing a centralized, transparent, and interactive space for data sharing, communication, and coordination, these platforms empower stakeholders to co-create, implement, and sustain impactful NBS projects.

1. The Role of Digital Platforms in NBS Governance

Digital platforms serve as a foundation for collaborative governance, enabling diverse stakeholders to work together efficiently. These platforms integrate data, tools, and communication channels to streamline decision-making and project management.

a. Centralized Data Repository

Digital platforms act as a centralized repository for all data related to NBS projects, including environmental metrics, stakeholder inputs, and project outcomes:

• **Real-Time Access:** Stakeholders, such as government agencies, NGOs, local communities, and private investors, can access up-to-date information on project progress and performance.

• **Data Transparency:** A shared database ensures that all stakeholders have equal access to critical information, fostering trust and accountability.

For instance, in a wetland restoration project, a digital platform might provide data on water quality, biodiversity, and community contributions, ensuring transparency in resource allocation and impact tracking.

b. Integration of Tools and Technologies

Digital platforms integrate various technologies, such as GIS, IoT devices, and AI, to support NBS governance:

• GIS visualizes spatial data, helping stakeholders understand geographical dynamics and prioritize interventions.

• IoT devices feed real-time data into the platform, enabling continuous monitoring of ecosystems.

• AI analyzes large datasets to generate insights and predict outcomes, guiding evidence-based decisions.

c. Collaborative Decision-Making

Digital platforms enable participatory governance by allowing stakeholders to contribute to decision-making processes. For example:

• Governments can use platforms to solicit input from local communities on urban green infrastructure projects.

• Farmers and landowners can collaborate with environmental agencies to design agroforestry systems that balance productivity with conservation.

2. Fostering Stakeholder Engagement Through Digital Platforms

Engaging stakeholders effectively is critical for ensuring the success and sustainability of NBS. Digital platforms provide interactive features and tools that enhance communication, education, and collaboration.

a. Interactive Communication Channels

Digital platforms facilitate seamless communication among stakeholders, overcoming geographical and logistical barriers:

• **Discussion Forums:** Stakeholders can participate in virtual forums to share ideas, raise concerns, and provide feedback.

• **Video Conferencing and Webinars:** Platforms enable remote meetings and training sessions, ensuring that stakeholders remain informed and engaged.

• **Instant Messaging and Notifications:** Real-time communication keeps stakeholders updated on project developments and upcoming activities.

For example, in a reforestation project, a digital platform might host webinars on sustainable land management practices, engaging local farmers and community members.

b. Educational Resources

Digital platforms provide educational tools and resources to enhance stakeholder understanding of NBS and their benefits:

• **Data Visualizations:** Interactive maps, graphs, and dashboards help stakeholders interpret complex data and understand project impacts.

• **E-Learning Modules:** Online courses and tutorials educate stakeholders about ecosystem dynamics, conservation practices, and the role of NBS in addressing climate challenges.

• **Case Studies and Reports:** Access to success stories and best practices inspires stakeholders and provides actionable insights for their own projects.

By empowering stakeholders with knowledge, digital platforms ensure informed participation and ownership of NBS initiatives.

c. Community Participation and Crowdsourcing

Digital platforms engage local communities by enabling participatory data collection and decision-making:

• **Citizen Science Projects:** Community members can contribute data through mobile apps, such as reporting wildlife sightings or uploading photos of environmental changes.

• **Polls and Surveys:** Platforms allow communities to vote on project priorities, such as selecting tree species for urban parks or identifying areas for flood mitigation.

• **Feedback Mechanisms:** Stakeholders can provide feedback on ongoing projects, ensuring that interventions align with local needs and expectations.

For instance, a coastal restoration project might use a digital platform to involve fishermen in monitoring marine biodiversity, fostering collaboration and trust.

3. Advantages of Digital Platforms for NBS Governance

Digital platforms offer several advantages that make them indispensable for collaborative governance and stakeholder engagement in NBS projects.

a. Transparency and Accountability

By providing a shared space for data and communication, digital platforms ensure that decisions and actions are transparent:

• Financial transactions, resource allocations, and project outcomes are recorded and accessible to all stakeholders.

• Stakeholders can track progress against agreed-upon milestones and hold one another accountable for their commitments.

b. Efficiency and Scalability

Digital platforms streamline governance processes, enabling stakeholders to collaborate more efficiently:

• Automated workflows, such as smart contracts, reduce administrative burdens and accelerate decision-making.

• The scalability of digital platforms makes them suitable for managing large-scale or multi-site NBS projects.

c. Inclusivity and Equity

Digital platforms promote inclusivity by giving all stakeholders, including marginalized groups, an equal voice in governance:

• Remote access ensures that stakeholders in rural or underserved areas can participate in decision-making.

• Language translation and accessibility features make platforms user-friendly for diverse audiences.

d. Adaptive Management

By integrating real-time data and predictive tools, digital platforms support adaptive management of NBS:

• Stakeholders can respond quickly to changes in environmental conditions or project performance.

• Continuous feedback loops enable iterative improvements, ensuring long-term sustainability.

4. Challenges and Future Opportunities

While digital platforms offer significant benefits, challenges must be addressed to maximize their potential in NBS governance.

a. Challenges

• **Technical Barriers:** Developing and maintaining digital platforms requires technical expertise and infrastructure, which may be lacking in resource-constrained areas.

• **Digital Divide:** Ensuring that all stakeholders have access to the necessary devices, internet connectivity, and digital literacy is critical for inclusivity.

• **Data Privacy and Security:** Safeguarding sensitive data, such as community information or financial records, is essential to maintain trust.

b. Opportunities

• **Integration with Emerging Technologies:** Combining digital platforms with blockchain, AI, and IoT can enhance data accuracy, security, and scalability.

• **Open-Source Platforms:** Developing open-source solutions reduces costs and makes digital platforms more accessible to smaller organizations and communities.

• **Community-Driven Development:** Involving local stakeholders in the design of digital platforms ensures that tools align with their needs and preferences.

Ethical Considerations and Challenges in Using Data for NBS Governance

Data-driven approaches have become essential for the governance and implementation of NBS. However, the collection, processing, and use of data raise important ethical considerations and challenges that must be addressed to ensure equity, inclusivity, and transparency. These issues span data privacy, access disparities, biases in data representation, and the ethical implications of decision-making based on data. This section explores these challenges and offers insights into how they can be addressed to foster responsible and sustainable use of data in NBS governance.

1. Data Privacy and Security

The collection and use of data in NBS governance often involve sensitive information, including geographic, environmental, and community-level data. Ensuring the privacy and security of this data is critical to maintaining trust and preventing misuse.

a. Protecting Community Data

In many NBS projects, data is collected from local communities, including personal information and observations about environmental conditions. Ethical concerns arise when:

• **Privacy is not safeguarded:** Individuals may hesitate to participate if they fear that their personal information could be misused.

• **Consent is unclear:** Community members may not fully understand how their data will be used or shared, raising concerns about informed consent.

b. Preventing Unauthorized Access

Data breaches or unauthorized access to sensitive datasets can compromise the security of NBS projects and the communities they aim to benefit. For instance:

• Environmental data on vulnerable ecosystems could be exploited by entities with conflicting interests, such as developers or extractive industries.

• Community input on project priorities could be manipulated to influence governance decisions.

c. Mitigation Strategies

• **Encryption and Access Control:** Secure storage systems and access protocols can protect sensitive data from breaches.

• **Informed Consent Mechanisms:** Clear communication about data use and explicit consent processes ensure that individuals and communities understand and agree to data collection practices.

2. Inclusivity and Data Access

Ensuring that all stakeholders have equitable access to data is a fundamental ethical consideration in NBS governance. Disparities in access can exacerbate inequalities and limit the participation of marginalized groups.

a. Digital Divide

Many rural and underserved communities lack the infrastructure, tools, or digital literacy needed to access and use data-driven platforms. This creates barriers to their meaningful participation in NBS governance:

• Communities may be excluded from decision-making processes due to a lack of access to digital tools or reliable internet.

• Stakeholders in remote areas may not have access to real-time environmental data, limiting their ability to contribute effectively.

b. Language and Cultural Barriers

Data representation and communication often fail to consider linguistic and cultural differences. For example:

• Data visualizations and technical reports may be inaccessible to non-experts or individuals who do not speak the primary language of the platform.

• Traditional ecological knowledge, which is vital for NBS, may not be captured or represented adequately in data systems.

c. Mitigation Strategies

• **Capacity Building:** Training programs can empower communities with the skills and knowledge needed to engage with data platforms.

• **Localized Tools:** Platforms should offer multilingual support, intuitive interfaces, and culturally relevant data representations.

• **Inclusive Data Sharing:** Providing offline access to data and ensuring affordability of tools, such as mobile apps, can bridge access gaps.

3. Bias in Data Collection and Analysis

Biases in data collection, representation, and analysis can undermine the effectiveness and equity of NBS governance. These biases often stem from systemic inequalities or flawed methodologies.

a. Skewed Data Representation

Data collected for NBS projects may disproportionately reflect the priorities of certain stakeholders, such as government agencies or private investors, while sidelining community perspectives. For example:

• Biodiversity data may focus on high-profile species while neglecting less visible but ecologically significant organisms.

• Environmental data may prioritize urban areas over rural landscapes, perpetuating inequalities in resource allocation.

b. Algorithmic Bias

The algorithms used to analyze data can inadvertently reinforce existing biases. For instance:

• Predictive models may rely on incomplete or historically biased datasets, leading to skewed recommendations.

• Automated decision-making systems may fail to account for local knowledge or context-specific factors.

c. Mitigation Strategies

• **Diversified Data Sources:** Including data from community members, traditional knowledge systems, and underrepresented regions ensures a more holistic perspective.

• **Bias Audits:** Regularly evaluating and addressing biases in data collection and analysis improves the accuracy and fairness of insights.

• **Participatory Methodologies:** Involving diverse stakeholders in the design of data collection and analysis processes fosters inclusivity.

4. Ethical Decision-Making Based on Data

Relying on data to make governance decisions in NBS projects raises ethical questions about accountability, transparency, and the potential misuse of data.

a. Over-Reliance on Data

While data-driven approaches enhance decision-making, over-reliance on quantitative metrics can marginalize qualitative inputs, such as community feedback or cultural values. For example:

• A wetland restoration project may prioritize cost-effectiveness based on data models, overlooking the social or spiritual significance of certain areas to local communities.

b. Transparency in Decision-Making

Ethical concerns arise when stakeholders lack visibility into how data is used to inform decisions. For instance:

• Communities may not understand why certain areas were prioritized for interventions or why specific strategies were chosen.

• Private investors or donors may question the credibility of reported outcomes if the data and methodologies used are not transparent.

c. Mitigation Strategies

• **Balanced Decision-Making:** Combining quantitative data with qualitative insights ensures that decisions reflect both scientific and social considerations.

• **Transparent Reporting:** Clear communication of data sources, methodologies, and decision-making processes fosters trust among stakeholders.

• **Ethical Frameworks:** Establishing guidelines for the ethical use of data ensures accountability and inclusivity in governance.

5. Emerging Opportunities to Address Ethical Challenges

Despite these challenges, advancements in technology and collaboration offer opportunities to enhance the ethical use of data in NBS governance:

a. Open-Source Platforms

Open-source data platforms promote transparency and inclusivity by providing free access to tools and datasets, enabling broader participation.

b. Community-Led Data Initiatives

Empowering communities to lead data collection and analysis ensures that their perspectives and priorities are reflected in governance decisions.

c. Ethical AI and Automation

Developing AI systems that prioritize fairness, accountability, and transparency reduces the risks of algorithmic bias and misuse.

d. Collaborative Governance Models

Partnerships among governments, NGOs, private entities, and local communities create shared accountability for ethical data use.

Chapter 8: Enhancing Community Engagement Through Digital Tools

Community engagement is a cornerstone of successful NBS. By involving local communities in the planning, implementation, and management of NBS projects, stakeholders can ensure that interventions are inclusive, sustainable, and aligned with local needs. Digital tools offer innovative ways to enhance this engagement, breaking down barriers to participation and fostering collaboration.

This chapter explores how digital technologies—such as mobile apps, VR, and crowdsourcing platforms—empower communities to actively contribute to NBS projects. It highlights the benefits of using digital tools for co-creation, education, and data collection, while addressing challenges such as digital access, inclusivity, and data privacy. Through these tools, communities can become key partners in driving climate resilience and sustainability.

Use of Apps, Virtual Reality, and Augmented Reality to Engage Communities in Nature-Based Solutions

Community engagement is vital for the success of NBS, as it ensures local buy-in, leverages local knowledge, and fosters a sense of stewardship. In an increasingly digital world, innovative technologies like mobile apps, VR, and Augmented Reality (AR) provide powerful tools to engage communities in NBS projects. These tools not only enhance awareness and understanding but also empower individuals and groups to actively participate in the design, implementation, and monitoring of NBS. This section explores the transformative potential of these technologies in fostering meaningful community engagement.

1. Mobile Apps for Accessibility and Participation

Mobile apps are a highly accessible tool for engaging communities in NBS, enabling individuals to contribute to projects, access educational resources, and monitor progress in real time. These apps leverage the ubiquity of smartphones to bridge the gap between stakeholders and on-the-ground participants.

a. Citizen Science and Data Collection

Mobile apps enable communities to contribute valuable data to NBS projects:

• **Crowdsourcing Environmental Data:** Apps allow users to upload photos, report environmental changes, or log observations of local flora and fauna. For instance, an app for reforestation might let users track tree growth or report pest infestations.

• **Water Quality Monitoring:** In watershed management projects, communities can use apps to test and report water quality metrics, such as pH levels or turbidity, using simple testing kits integrated with app functionalities.

b. Real-Time Feedback and Updates

Apps provide a platform for real-time communication between project managers and community members:

• Project updates, such as milestones achieved or changes in project plans, can be shared instantly with all stakeholders.

• Communities can provide feedback through app features like surveys or discussion forums, ensuring that their voices are heard.

c. Gamification to Drive Engagement

Gamification features in apps incentivize community participation:

• Leaderboards and rewards systems encourage users to contribute more frequently, such as logging wildlife sightings or planting trees.

• Interactive challenges, like identifying local plant species or participating in clean-up events, make NBS projects engaging and educational.

2. VR for Immersive Education and Advocacy

VR technology provides an immersive experience that allows users to visualize and interact with NBS in ways that traditional methods cannot. VR is particularly effective for educating communities about the benefits of NBS and fostering advocacy for their implementation.

a. Visualizing Ecosystem Dynamics

VR allows users to explore ecosystems and understand how NBS interventions can transform them:

• **Before-and-After Scenarios:** A VR simulation of a degraded wetland and its restored state helps communities see the tangible benefits of the project, such as improved biodiversity and flood control.

• **Interactive Ecosystems:** Users can explore virtual forests, rivers, or coral reefs, learning about their ecological roles and the impacts of human activities.

b. Training and Capacity Building

VR simulations are a powerful tool for training local stakeholders in NBS practices:

• Farmers can use VR to learn sustainable agroforestry techniques or water management practices.

• Community members can be trained in planting methods, maintenance protocols, or wildlife monitoring through interactive VR tutorials.

c. Advocacy and Awareness Campaigns

VR experiences are an impactful way to raise awareness and advocate for NBS projects:

• Immersive storytelling in VR can take users on a journey through a threatened ecosystem, highlighting the urgency of intervention and the benefits of proposed solutions.

• Schools and community centers can use VR experiences to educate younger generations about the importance of conservation and restoration efforts.

3. AR for On-the-Ground Engagement

AR overlays digital information onto the physical world, enabling real-time interaction with NBS projects. This technology is particularly effective for engaging communities in urban environments, where space and resources may be limited.

a. Interactive Project Planning

AR tools enable communities to participate in the planning of NBS projects:

• **Visualizing Proposed Changes:** An AR app can show users how a park or green roof will look once completed, helping them understand the project's impact and offer informed feedback.

• **Design Customization:** Community members can use AR to suggest design elements, such as the placement of trees, benches, or walking paths in a new green space.

b. Real-Time Learning and Exploration

AR apps provide on-the-spot education about ecosystems and NBS interventions:

• **Interactive Guides:** Users can point their smartphone cameras at plants, animals, or geographic features to learn about their ecological roles. For example, an AR app might identify a tree species and explain its carbon sequestration potential.

• **Trail Experiences:** In nature reserves or urban green spaces, AR guides can offer real-time information about restoration efforts, biodiversity, and ecosystem services.

c. Encouraging Community Stewardship

AR tools foster a sense of ownership and responsibility among community members:

• **Maintenance Guidance:** AR overlays can show users how to maintain a green roof, care for a rain garden, or monitor a forest plot, empowering them to contribute to project upkeep.

• **Recognition of Contributions:** Community efforts, such as tree planting or litter collection, can be highlighted through AR, with virtual badges or markers acknowledging individual or group contributions.

4. Benefits of Using Digital Tools for Community Engagement

The use of apps, VR, and AR in NBS projects offers numerous benefits for communities and stakeholders:

a. Increased Awareness and Understanding

These tools make complex ecological concepts accessible, helping communities understand the importance and benefits of NBS.

b. Enhanced Participation

By making engagement interactive, educational, and rewarding, digital tools encourage more people to actively participate in NBS projects.

c. Real-Time Collaboration

Digital tools facilitate seamless communication and collaboration among stakeholders, ensuring that projects align with community needs and priorities.

d. Building Long-Term Stewardship

By empowering communities to contribute to and learn from NBS projects, these technologies foster a sense of ownership and responsibility for their success.

5. Challenges and Future Directions

While digital tools hold immense potential, challenges must be addressed to maximize their impact:

Challenges

• **Digital Divide:** Limited access to smartphones, VR equipment, or reliable internet can exclude underserved communities.

• **Technical Complexity:** Designing and maintaining these tools requires technical expertise and resources.

• **Privacy Concerns:** Collecting and using community data through digital tools must respect privacy and consent.

Future Directions

• **Affordable Solutions:** Developing low-cost and open-source digital tools can make these technologies more accessible to resource-constrained communities.

• **Localized Content:** Customizing tools to reflect local languages, cultures, and ecological conditions enhances their relevance and effectiveness.

• **Integration with Traditional Practices:** Combining digital tools with traditional community engagement methods ensures inclusivity and broader participation.

Crowdsourcing Data and Citizen Science as Tools for Co-Creation in Nature-Based Solutions

The success of NBS often hinges on the participation of local communities in their design, implementation, and management. Crowdsourcing data and citizen science are two powerful approaches that enable communities to contribute directly to NBS projects, fostering co-creation and ownership. These methods leverage collective knowledge, observations, and expertise to provide valuable insights, enhance stakeholder engagement, and improve project outcomes. This section explores how crowdsourcing and citizen science are transforming NBS by integrating diverse perspectives and empowering communities.

1. Understanding Crowdsourcing and Citizen Science

a. Crowdsourcing Data

Crowdsourcing involves collecting data, ideas, or resources from a large group of people, typically through digital platforms such as mobile apps or websites. In the context of NBS, crowdsourcing allows individuals and communities to share observations about their local environment, such as changes in biodiversity, water quality, or vegetation cover.

b. Citizen Science

Citizen science involves public participation in scientific research, enabling non-experts to contribute to data collection, analysis, and even hypothesis generation. Citizen science projects often use structured protocols to ensure the quality and reliability of data.

c. Synergy Between Crowdsourcing and Citizen Science

While crowdsourcing focuses on gathering diverse inputs, citizen science emphasizes structured collaboration with communities. Together, these approaches enable co-creation, where communities play an active role in shaping NBS projects.

2. Applications in Co-Creating Nature-Based Solutions

Crowdsourcing data and citizen science have been successfully applied across various NBS contexts, from urban green infrastructure to biodiversity conservation and watershed management.

a. Biodiversity Monitoring

Community members can contribute observations of plants, animals, and ecosystems, enhancing biodiversity assessments for NBS projects:

• **Mobile Apps for Species Tracking:** Apps like iNaturalist enable users to upload photos of species, which are then identified and logged in global biodiversity databases. These observations inform the planning of green corridors, reforestation efforts, and protected areas.

• **Community-Led Surveys:** Local communities conduct surveys of flora and fauna, providing data that complements scientific assessments and highlights underrepresented areas.

b. Urban Green Infrastructure

In cities, crowdsourcing and citizen science engage residents in monitoring and improving urban ecosystems:

• **Heat Island Mapping:** Residents use mobile apps to measure temperature variations across neighborhoods, guiding the placement of green roofs, parks, and tree-lined streets to mitigate urban heat islands.

• **Air Quality Monitoring:** Community-driven air quality measurements identify pollution hotspots, informing the design of urban green spaces to improve air filtration and public health.

c. Watershed Management

Communities contribute data on water quality, flow, and usage, supporting NBS for watershed protection:

• **Water Quality Testing Kits:** Citizen scientists use affordable testing kits to measure parameters like pH, turbidity, and nutrient levels, providing data for wetland restoration and riparian buffer projects.

• **Flood Risk Mapping:** Residents share observations of flood-prone areas and historical flood patterns, helping identify priority sites for floodplain restoration or rainwater harvesting systems.

3. Benefits of Crowdsourcing and Citizen Science in NBS

a. Leveraging Local Knowledge

Local communities possess valuable insights about their environments, often based on years of lived experience:

• Farmers understand seasonal changes in soil and vegetation, which informs agroforestry and sustainable agriculture projects.

• Coastal residents are familiar with erosion patterns and storm impacts, guiding the restoration of mangroves or dunes.

By integrating this knowledge, NBS projects become more context-specific and effective.

b. Expanding Data Collection

Traditional scientific methods can be resource-intensive and limited in scope. Crowdsourcing and citizen science dramatically expand data collection efforts by mobilizing large numbers of participants:

• Observations from diverse locations provide a comprehensive view of ecosystems, including areas that might otherwise go unmonitored.

• Real-time data inputs allow for dynamic tracking of environmental changes, improving adaptive management.

c. Fostering Community Ownership

When communities actively contribute to NBS projects, they develop a sense of ownership and responsibility:

• Citizen science projects that involve planting and monitoring trees in reforestation efforts create long-term stewards for those ecosystems.

• Crowdsourcing platforms that enable residents to vote on project priorities, such as tree species selection or park design, build trust and support.

d. Promoting Environmental Education

Participating in data collection and monitoring deepens participants' understanding of ecological systems and the benefits of NBS:

• School-based citizen science programs engage students in biodiversity monitoring, cultivating a generation of environmentally conscious citizens.

• Workshops and training sessions provide community members with skills in data collection, analysis, and NBS maintenance.

4. Challenges and Solutions

While crowdsourcing and citizen science offer significant benefits, challenges must be addressed to maximize their potential.

a. Data Quality and Reliability

Concerns about the accuracy and consistency of data collected by non-experts are common:

• **Solution:** Providing clear protocols and training ensures that participants collect reliable data. For example, citizen science projects can use standardized methods and mobile apps with built-in quality controls, such as photo verification or automatic geotagging.

b. Accessibility and Inclusivity

Not all communities have access to the necessary tools or resources to participate:

• **Solution:** Developing low-cost, offline-compatible tools and providing devices, such as mobile phones or testing kits, ensures broader participation. Offering multilingual support and tailoring platforms to local contexts enhances inclusivity.

c. Sustaining Engagement

Maintaining long-term participation in crowdsourcing and citizen science projects can be challenging:

• **Solution:** Gamification, rewards, and recognition programs motivate participants to stay involved. For example, apps can award badges or points for contributions, fostering friendly competition and community pride.

d. Ethical Considerations

Ensuring data privacy and obtaining informed consent are critical:

• **Solution:** Transparent communication about data use and clear opt-in processes build trust. Platforms must comply with data protection regulations and respect community ownership of shared information.

5. Future Opportunities

The integration of emerging technologies and innovative approaches can further enhance the role of crowdsourcing and citizen science in NBS:

a. Integration with Digital Tools

Combining crowdsourcing and citizen science with IoT sensors, remote sensing, and AI enables more accurate and scalable data collection. For example:

• IoT sensors installed in community gardens can provide continuous data on soil moisture and temperature, complementing citizen observations.

b. Collaborative Platforms

Developing open-source platforms for crowdsourcing and citizen science fosters global collaboration and knowledge sharing. For instance:

• Regional citizen science networks can exchange data and insights, supporting cross-border NBS projects like migratory wildlife corridors or river basin restoration.

c. Policy Integration

Incorporating community-generated data into policy and planning frameworks ensures that local voices are heard. For example:

• Governments can use crowdsourced flood risk maps to prioritize funding for NBS projects in vulnerable areas.

Overcoming Barriers to Digital Inclusivity in Community Engagement for Nature-Based Solutions

Digital tools have revolutionized the way communities engage with NBS, offering platforms for education, collaboration, and participation. However, not all communities have equal access to these tools, leading to a digital divide that can exclude marginalized groups from fully participating in NBS projects. Overcoming barriers to digital inclusivity is essential for ensuring equitable access and fostering broad community involvement. This section explores key challenges to digital inclusivity in NBS engagement and outlines strategies to address them.

1. Understanding the Barriers to Digital Inclusivity

Digital inclusivity challenges arise from a combination of technological, economic, cultural, and educational factors. Identifying these barriers is the first step toward designing inclusive solutions.

a. Limited Access to Technology

Access to devices such as smartphones, computers, and IoT-enabled sensors is unevenly distributed, particularly in rural or low-income areas:

• Households may lack the financial resources to afford these devices.

• Infrastructure limitations, such as unreliable electricity or internet connectivity, further exacerbate the problem.

b. Internet Connectivity Gaps

Stable and affordable internet access is essential for leveraging digital tools, yet many regions face significant connectivity challenges:

• Remote and rural areas often have limited broadband coverage.

• High costs of internet access can exclude low-income groups.

c. Digital Literacy

Even when technology is available, a lack of digital literacy prevents many people from effectively using digital tools:

• Older generations and individuals with limited education may struggle with app interfaces or online platforms.

• Communities unfamiliar with digital tools may require additional training to participate meaningfully.

d. Cultural and Linguistic Barriers

Digital tools are often designed with a one-size-fits-all approach that fails to consider local cultural and linguistic contexts:

• Platforms may not support local languages, excluding non-native speakers.

• Content that is not culturally relevant or sensitive can alienate communities.

2. Strategies for Overcoming Barriers

To ensure inclusive community engagement, stakeholders must implement strategies that address these challenges and promote equitable access to digital tools.

a. Expanding Access to Technology

Providing communities with affordable and accessible digital tools is critical:

• **Low-Cost Devices:** Partnerships with technology providers can offer subsidized or donated devices, such as smartphones or tablets, to underserved communities.

• **Shared Resources:** Community centers or local schools can host shared digital hubs equipped with computers and internet access.

• **Solar-Powered Solutions:** In areas with unreliable electricity, solar-powered charging stations ensure consistent access to devices.

b. Improving Internet Connectivity

Efforts to bridge connectivity gaps focus on making internet access more reliable and affordable:

• **Community Networks:** Localized networks, such as Wi-Fi hotspots in public areas, can extend coverage to underserved regions.

• **Government Subsidies:** Policies that subsidize internet costs for low-income households ensure broader access.

• **Offline Functionality:** Designing digital tools with offline capabilities allows users to download content or input data without continuous connectivity.

c. Building Digital Literacy

Training programs tailored to the needs of specific communities can enhance digital literacy:

• **Workshops and Tutorials:** Hands-on training sessions teach users how to navigate apps, input data, and engage with online platforms.

• **Peer Support Networks:** Establishing local digital ambassadors who can mentor their peers fosters sustainable capacity-building.

• **Multimedia Learning Materials:** Visual aids, videos, and interactive guides simplify complex concepts and make learning accessible to all.

d. Designing Inclusive Platforms

Ensuring that digital tools are user-friendly and culturally appropriate promotes inclusivity:

• **Localized Content:** Platforms should support multiple languages and use visuals or audio cues to communicate with users who have limited literacy.

• **Customizable Interfaces:** Simplified, intuitive interfaces allow users with varying skill levels to engage effectively.

• **Culturally Relevant Features:** Including culturally specific examples, symbols, or narratives enhances the relatability of tools.

3. Engaging Marginalized Groups

Marginalized groups, including women, indigenous communities, and people with disabilities, often face additional barriers to digital engagement. Targeted interventions are necessary to ensure their inclusion in NBS projects.

a. Women's Empowerment

In many societies, women face systemic challenges in accessing technology and participating in decision-making:

• **Access Programs:** Initiatives that provide women with devices, training, and internet access empower them to engage in NBS projects.

• **Safe Spaces:** Creating gender-sensitive environments for training and collaboration encourages women's participation.

b. Indigenous Communities

Indigenous knowledge is invaluable for NBS, yet these communities are often excluded from digital initiatives:

• **Co-Creation of Tools:** Collaborating with indigenous leaders to design digital platforms ensures that their perspectives and needs are integrated.

• **Recognition of Traditional Knowledge:** Platforms should value and incorporate indigenous ecological knowledge as a critical data source.

c. Accessibility for People with Disabilities

Digital tools must be designed to accommodate users with disabilities:

• **Assistive Technologies:** Features such as screen readers, voice commands, and tactile feedback make tools accessible to users with visual, auditory, or physical impairments.

• **Universal Design:** Ensuring platforms adhere to universal design principles benefits all users, including those with varying abilities.

4. Benefits of Digital Inclusivity in NBS Engagement

Overcoming barriers to digital inclusivity yields significant benefits for NBS projects and the communities they serve:

a. Broader Participation

Inclusive digital tools enable more people to contribute to NBS projects, enriching the pool of ideas, knowledge, and resources.

b. Enhanced Community Ownership

When communities feel empowered to engage meaningfully, they are more likely to take ownership of NBS initiatives, ensuring long-term sustainability.

c. Improved Data Quality

Diverse contributions from a wide range of participants result in richer, more accurate datasets for monitoring and decision-making.

d. Social Equity

Digital inclusivity promotes fairness and equity by ensuring that marginalized groups have a voice in environmental governance.

5. Future Directions for Digital Inclusivity

Advancing digital inclusivity requires continued innovation and collaboration among governments, NGOs, private sector actors, and local communities:

a. Public-Private Partnerships

Partnerships with tech companies can drive the development of affordable, inclusive digital tools and infrastructure.

b. Open-Source Solutions

Open-source platforms democratize access to digital tools, allowing communities to adapt them to their specific needs.

c. Policy Support

Governments play a crucial role in creating policies that promote digital equity, such as subsidies for internet access or funding for digital literacy programs.

d. Monitoring and Evaluation

Regularly assessing the inclusivity and impact of digital tools ensures continuous improvement and alignment with community needs.

Chapter 9: Scaling Up Nature-Based Solutions Through Digital Innovation

NBS offer transformative potential to address global challenges such as climate change, biodiversity loss, and water security. However, scaling up these solutions to broader landscapes and populations requires innovative approaches that harness the power of digital technology. Digital tools and platforms enable efficient planning, implementation, monitoring, and replication of NBS, bridging gaps in resources, knowledge, and governance.

This chapter explores the role of digital innovation in scaling up NBS. It highlights key strategies such as leveraging big data, cloud computing, and advanced analytics to support large-scale projects. Additionally, it examines the importance of partnerships between technology providers and environmental organizations in achieving scalable, impactful solutions. By integrating digital tools into NBS frameworks, stakeholders can ensure that these interventions deliver widespread benefits for ecosystems and communities alike.

Strategies for Scaling Up Nature-Based Solutions Using Digital Platforms and Technologies

Scaling up NBS to address global environmental challenges requires innovative strategies that go beyond localized interventions. Digital platforms and technologies offer powerful tools to expand the reach, efficiency, and impact of NBS. These tools enable stakeholders to optimize planning, streamline implementation, monitor progress, and foster collaboration across regions and sectors. By leveraging digital innovations, NBS can be implemented at larger scales, delivering more significant benefits for ecosystems, economies, and societies.

1. Leveraging Big Data for Informed Decision-Making

Big data plays a central role in scaling up NBS by providing the comprehensive insights needed for effective planning and management. Large datasets collected from satellites, IoT devices, and citizen science initiatives help stakeholders understand complex ecological systems and design interventions that maximize impact.

a. Ecosystem Analysis and Mapping

• **Spatial Analysis:** Digital platforms that integrate big data and GIS allow for detailed mapping of ecosystems, identifying priority areas for NBS interventions such as reforestation, wetland restoration, or coral reef conservation.

• **Risk Assessments:** By analyzing historical and real-time data, stakeholders can identify regions most vulnerable to climate impacts such as flooding, drought, or heatwaves, guiding the strategic placement of NBS.

b. Predictive Modeling

• Predictive models powered by big data simulate the potential outcomes of NBS at scale, helping decision-makers anticipate the long-term impacts of interventions.

• For example, models can forecast how large-scale reforestation efforts will influence regional water cycles, biodiversity, and carbon sequestration.

c. Data-Driven Prioritization

• Big data enables the prioritization of NBS projects by evaluating ecological, social, and economic benefits across different scenarios.

• For instance, stakeholders can use data to prioritize urban green infrastructure projects that provide the most significant cooling effects or flood protection in densely populated areas.

2. Harnessing Cloud Computing for Scalability

Cloud computing offers the computational power and storage capacity needed to scale up NBS efficiently. By hosting data, tools, and platforms in the cloud, stakeholders can collaborate, analyze, and implement projects across multiple regions.

a. Centralized Data Repositories

• Cloud-based platforms act as centralized repositories for environmental data, ensuring that all stakeholders have access to consistent, up-to-date information.

• Shared repositories facilitate cross-border collaboration on transnational NBS projects, such as river basin management or migratory wildlife corridors.

b. Real-Time Data Processing

• Cloud computing enables the real-time processing of large datasets, allowing for dynamic monitoring and adaptive management of NBS.

• For example, IoT sensors in wetlands or forests can feed data into cloud platforms, providing instant insights into ecosystem health and intervention effectiveness.

c. Cost-Effective Scalability

• Cloud-based solutions eliminate the need for costly local infrastructure, making it easier for smaller organizations and resource-constrained regions to participate in large-scale NBS initiatives.

3. Digital Platforms for Collaborative Planning and Governance

Digital platforms designed for collaborative planning and governance are instrumental in scaling up NBS. These platforms enable stakeholders to coordinate efforts, share resources, and engage communities effectively.

a. Multi-Stakeholder Collaboration

• Platforms like project management tools and decision-support systems bring together governments, NGOs, private sector actors, and local communities to design and implement NBS collaboratively.

• For example, a platform for urban green infrastructure projects might allow city planners, residents, and environmental experts to co-create park designs or tree-planting initiatives.

b. Participatory Governance

• Digital platforms that incorporate features like voting, surveys, and discussion forums enable inclusive decision-making, ensuring that community voices are heard in large-scale NBS projects.

• For instance, residents in flood-prone areas can use these platforms to prioritize interventions such as floodplain restoration or rainwater harvesting systems.

c. Transparent Reporting

• Platforms that provide transparent updates on project progress, funding, and outcomes foster trust and accountability among stakeholders.

• For example, blockchain-enabled platforms can track the flow of funds in reforestation projects, ensuring that resources are allocated equitably and effectively.

4. Advanced Analytics for Optimized Interventions

Advanced analytics, powered by AI and ML, enhance the scalability of NBS by optimizing resource allocation, monitoring, and management.

a. Resource Optimization

• AI-driven algorithms analyze large datasets to identify the most cost-effective and impactful NBS interventions.

• For example, machine learning models can determine the ideal mix of tree species for large-scale reforestation efforts, maximizing biodiversity and carbon sequestration.

b. Ecosystem Monitoring

• Advanced analytics process data from IoT sensors, drones, and satellite imagery to monitor ecosystems at scale, detecting changes in vegetation, water quality, or wildlife populations.

• These insights enable stakeholders to adapt management strategies in real-time, ensuring that NBS remain effective under changing conditions.

c. Risk Mitigation

• Predictive analytics identify potential risks to large-scale NBS projects, such as pest outbreaks, extreme weather events, or human disturbances.

• By anticipating challenges, stakeholders can implement proactive measures, such as pest control programs or protective barriers, to safeguard NBS investments.

5. Community Engagement Through Digital Innovation

Scaling up NBS requires active community involvement, which can be facilitated through digital tools designed for education, participation, and stewardship.

a. Mobile Apps for Participation

• Mobile apps enable communities to contribute to large-scale NBS projects by sharing observations, providing feedback, and participating in data collection.

• For example, an app for urban reforestation might allow residents to suggest tree planting locations or report maintenance needs.

b. VR and AR

• VR and AR technologies engage communities by visualizing the benefits of large-scale NBS projects, fostering understanding and support.

• For instance, a VR simulation of a restored mangrove forest can demonstrate its protective effects against storm surges, inspiring community involvement.

c. Crowdsourcing Platforms

• Crowdsourcing platforms enable large-scale participation in data collection and monitoring, leveraging the collective knowledge and efforts of diverse stakeholders.

• For example, a platform for watershed management might allow users to report water quality metrics or map erosion hotspots.

6. Building Partnerships for Scale

Collaborative partnerships between technology providers, environmental organizations, and governments are essential for scaling up NBS using digital innovations.

a. Public-Private Partnerships

• Partnerships between governments and tech companies can fund and develop the digital infrastructure needed for large-scale NBS projects.

• For instance, a partnership might create a national platform for tracking urban green infrastructure performance across multiple cities.

b. Cross-Sector Collaboration

• Environmental NGOs, academic institutions, and private companies can collaborate to integrate scientific expertise, technological innovation, and financial resources.

• For example, a collaborative effort might combine AI research from universities with corporate funding to scale up biodiversity conservation efforts.

c. Capacity Building

• Partnerships that invest in capacity building ensure that local stakeholders have the skills and tools needed to implement and manage NBS at scale.

The Role of Cloud Computing and Big Data Analytics in Supporting Larger Nature-Based Solutions Projects

Scaling up NBS to address global environmental challenges requires powerful tools for managing vast amounts of data and coordinating complex processes. Cloud computing and big data analytics play pivotal roles in enabling the efficient design, implementation, and monitoring of large-scale NBS projects. Together, these technologies provide the computational capacity, storage, and analytical capabilities needed to optimize decision-making, enhance collaboration, and maximize the impact of NBS.

1. Leveraging Cloud Computing for Scalability and Collaboration

Cloud computing provides a flexible and scalable platform for managing the extensive data and workflows associated with large NBS projects. By hosting data, tools, and applications in a cloud environment, stakeholders can collaborate efficiently, access real-time information, and scale operations as needed.

a. Centralized Data Management

Large-scale NBS projects involve data from multiple sources, including satellite imagery, IoT sensors, and field surveys. Cloud computing enables centralized storage and management of this data, ensuring consistency and accessibility:

• **Single Source of Truth:** A cloud-based repository serves as a unified source of information for all stakeholders, reducing duplication and errors.

• **Data Integration:** Cloud platforms allow for the seamless integration of diverse datasets, such as biodiversity metrics, water quality data, and land-use maps, facilitating holistic analysis.

For example, a cloud-based platform for watershed restoration can integrate hydrological models, climate data, and community inputs, providing stakeholders with a comprehensive view of the project.

b. Real-Time Data Access

Cloud computing enables stakeholders to access and share data in real time, enhancing decision-making and coordination:

• **Dynamic Monitoring:** IoT sensors deployed in forests, wetlands, or urban green spaces send real-time data to the cloud, allowing for immediate analysis and response.

• **Collaborative Tools:** Cloud-based tools such as shared dashboards, project management software, and communication platforms support seamless collaboration among governments, NGOs, and communities.

For instance, a reforestation project can use a cloud-based dashboard to track tree planting progress, monitor ecosystem health, and coordinate activities across multiple sites.

c. Cost-Effective Scalability

Cloud computing offers cost-effective solutions for scaling up NBS projects:

• **On-Demand Resources:** Cloud platforms provide on-demand computational power and storage, eliminating the need for costly local infrastructure.

• **Pay-As-You-Go Models:** Flexible pricing models allow stakeholders to pay only for the resources they use, making cloud computing accessible to smaller organizations and resource-constrained regions.

2. Harnessing Big Data Analytics for Informed Decision-Making

Big data analytics transforms raw data into actionable insights, enabling stakeholders to design, implement, and manage NBS projects more effectively. By processing and analyzing vast datasets, big data analytics supports evidence-based decision-making and enhances the scalability of NBS.

a. Identifying Priority Areas

Big data analytics helps stakeholders identify priority areas for NBS interventions by analyzing environmental, social, and economic factors:

• **Spatial Analysis:** GIS and remote sensing data allow for the identification of degraded ecosystems, biodiversity hotspots, and climate-vulnerable regions.

• **Socioeconomic Metrics:** Analytics tools integrate data on population density, land use, and community needs to guide the placement of urban green spaces, flood mitigation projects, and other NBS.

For example, a big data platform can combine satellite imagery and socioeconomic data to prioritize reforestation efforts in areas with high erosion risk and significant community dependence on natural resources.

b. Predictive Modeling

Predictive analytics powered by machine learning and AI enables stakeholders to forecast the outcomes of NBS projects:

• **Climate Impact Simulations:** Models predict how large-scale NBS, such as mangrove restoration or afforestation, will influence local and regional climates, including rainfall patterns and temperature regulation.

- **Ecosystem Dynamics:** Predictive tools simulate how ecosystems will evolve under different scenarios, such as varying levels of human activity, climate change, or species reintroduction.

For instance, predictive models can forecast the carbon sequestration potential of a nationwide reforestation program, helping stakeholders set realistic targets and allocate resources effectively.

c. Adaptive Management

Big data analytics supports adaptive management by providing insights into the performance and impacts of NBS over time:

- **Performance Metrics:** Analytics tools process data from IoT sensors, drones, and field surveys to evaluate metrics such as tree growth, water quality, and biodiversity recovery.

- **Real-Time Adjustments:** Continuous monitoring and analysis enable stakeholders to identify challenges and implement corrective actions, such as adjusting irrigation schedules or addressing pest outbreaks.

For example, a wetland restoration project can use big data analytics to monitor nutrient levels and vegetation health, ensuring that the ecosystem continues to provide flood protection and water filtration services.

3. Synergies Between Cloud Computing and Big Data Analytics

The integration of cloud computing and big data analytics creates a powerful ecosystem for managing large-scale NBS projects. These technologies work together to enhance efficiency, scalability, and collaboration.

a. High-Performance Computing

Cloud platforms provide the computational power needed to process and analyze massive datasets in real time:

• For example, a nationwide urban greening initiative can use cloud-based analytics to assess air quality improvements across multiple cities simultaneously.

b. Seamless Data Integration

Cloud computing enables the integration of diverse datasets, while big data analytics extracts meaningful insights:

• For instance, a marine conservation project can combine satellite data on coral reef health with community-reported observations of fish populations to design targeted interventions.

c. Democratizing Access

By hosting data and tools in the cloud, stakeholders across regions and sectors can access advanced analytics capabilities without requiring specialized infrastructure:

• This democratization of technology ensures that smaller organizations and local communities can participate in large-scale NBS projects.

4. Challenges and Future Opportunities

While cloud computing and big data analytics offer immense potential for scaling up NBS, challenges remain:

Challenges

• **Data Accessibility:** Ensuring that all stakeholders, including marginalized communities, have access to cloud-based platforms and analytical tools is critical.

• **Data Quality:** The accuracy and reliability of big data depend on the quality of the input data, which may vary across sources.

• **Technical Expertise:** Using these technologies requires technical skills that may not be readily available in all regions or organizations.

Opportunities

• **Open-Source Platforms:** Developing open-source tools for cloud computing and big data analytics can reduce costs and increase accessibility.

• **Capacity Building:** Training programs can equip stakeholders with the skills needed to use these technologies effectively.

• **Integration with Emerging Technologies:** Combining cloud computing and big data analytics with AI, IoT, and blockchain can further enhance their capabilities for NBS management.

Insights on Partnerships Between Technology Providers and Environmental Organizations

Scaling up NBS to address global environmental challenges requires a collaborative approach that brings together diverse expertise and resources. Partnerships between technology providers and environmental organizations play a pivotal role in enabling these solutions. These partnerships combine cutting-edge technological capabilities with deep ecological knowledge to design, implement, and monitor NBS projects effectively. This section explores the dynamics, benefits, and challenges of such partnerships, providing insights into how they can drive impactful and scalable environmental solutions.

1. The Rationale for Partnerships

Technology providers and environmental organizations have complementary strengths that, when combined, can overcome many barriers to scaling up NBS.

a. Technology Providers: Catalysts for Innovation

Technology providers contribute advanced tools, platforms, and expertise essential for modernizing NBS:

• **Digital Platforms:** Providers offer software for data management, visualization, and collaboration, streamlining project planning and implementation.

• **Sensors and IoT Devices:** Technology companies supply monitoring tools that collect real-time environmental data, such as water quality, air pollution, and biodiversity metrics.

• **Advanced Analytics:** Machine learning, AI, and big data analytics enable detailed insights into ecosystem dynamics and intervention impacts.

b. Environmental Organizations: Stewards of Ecosystems

Environmental organizations bring ecological expertise, local knowledge, and community networks:

• **Ecological Understanding:** These organizations possess detailed knowledge of natural systems, ensuring that technology is applied in contextually appropriate ways.

• **Community Engagement:** Environmental organizations have established relationships with local communities, fostering trust and participation.

• **Conservation Goals:** Their mission-driven focus ensures that technology applications align with broader sustainability objectives.

c. The Synergy

By combining technological innovation with ecological stewardship, partnerships create integrated solutions that are both effective and sustainable. For example, a technology provider might develop an app for mapping urban green spaces, while an environmental NGO ensures that the app includes community-relevant features and ecological insights.

2. Key Areas of Collaboration

Collaborative partnerships between technology providers and environmental organizations span several critical areas that enhance the scalability and impact of NBS.

a. Data Collection and Monitoring

Real-time data is essential for managing large-scale NBS projects, and partnerships enable efficient data collection and monitoring:

• **IoT and Remote Sensing:** Technology providers offer IoT devices, drones, and satellites, while environmental organizations deploy these tools to monitor ecosystems.

• **Community-Generated Data:** Environmental organizations engage local communities in crowdsourcing data, which is then integrated into digital platforms developed by technology providers.

For instance, a partnership could involve installing IoT sensors in wetlands to monitor water quality, with data shared through a cloud platform accessible to all stakeholders.

b. Digital Platforms for Planning and Governance

Collaborative partnerships develop platforms that support participatory governance and project management:

• **Decision-Support Systems:** Technology providers create tools that analyze data and simulate scenarios, enabling stakeholders to make informed decisions.

• **Collaborative Interfaces:** Environmental organizations contribute design inputs to ensure that platforms are user-friendly and inclusive.

An example is a cloud-based platform that combines satellite imagery, predictive analytics, and community feedback to plan urban green infrastructure projects.

c. Capacity Building

Partnerships focus on building the technical capacity of environmental organizations and local communities:

• **Training Programs:** Technology providers offer workshops on using digital tools, such as GIS software or IoT devices, while environmental organizations facilitate community participation.

• **Localized Solutions:** Environmental organizations help adapt tools to local contexts, ensuring relevance and accessibility.

For example, a partnership might train farmers to use mobile apps for monitoring soil health and water availability, integrating this data into regional NBS planning.

d. Funding and Resource Mobilization

Collaborative partnerships can secure funding and resources for NBS projects:

• **Corporate Social Responsibility (CSR):** Technology providers may fund NBS initiatives as part of their CSR commitments.

• **Joint Grant Applications:** Partnerships strengthen funding proposals by combining technological and ecological expertise.

An example is a partnership where a technology provider contributes in-kind resources, such as software licenses, while an environmental NGO leverages its network to secure additional funding from international donors.

3. Benefits of Partnerships

Collaborations between technology providers and environmental organizations offer numerous benefits that amplify the reach and impact of NBS projects.

a. Enhanced Efficiency

• Advanced tools provided by technology partners streamline data collection, analysis, and reporting, reducing the time and effort required for NBS implementation.

• Automation and real-time monitoring enable adaptive management, ensuring that resources are allocated effectively.

b. Increased Scalability

• Partnerships allow small-scale projects to be replicated across larger areas or regions by leveraging digital platforms and cloud computing.

• The integration of predictive analytics enables stakeholders to anticipate challenges and scale interventions strategically.

c. Broader Community Engagement

• Technology enhances community participation through accessible digital tools, such as mobile apps and AR platforms.

• Environmental organizations ensure that engagement efforts are culturally sensitive and inclusive.

d. Strengthened Impact Measurement

• Data-driven insights enable stakeholders to quantify the ecological, social, and economic benefits of NBS, strengthening the case for continued investment.

• Transparent reporting fosters accountability and trust among donors, governments, and communities.

4. Challenges and Strategies for Success

While partnerships offer significant advantages, they also face challenges that must be addressed for long-term success.

a. Misaligned Objectives

• Technology providers may prioritize innovation and scalability, while environmental organizations focus on local ecological and social outcomes.

• **Strategy:** Establish shared goals and clear communication to align priorities and ensure mutual benefits.

b. Resource Imbalances

• Technology providers often bring more financial and technical resources, creating potential power imbalances.

• **Strategy:** Foster equitable partnerships by valuing the ecological expertise and community networks of environmental organizations.

c. Technological Complexity

• Advanced tools may be too complex for local stakeholders to use effectively without proper training.

• **Strategy:** Design user-friendly solutions and provide ongoing capacity-building programs to empower all participants.

d. Data Privacy and Security

• Collecting and sharing environmental and community data raises ethical concerns about privacy and security.

• **Strategy:** Implement robust data protection measures and transparent consent processes to address these issues.

5. Future Opportunities

As technology and environmental challenges continue to evolve, partnerships between technology providers and environmental organizations offer exciting opportunities:

a. Integration of Emerging Technologies

• Combining AI, blockchain, and IoT can enhance data accuracy, security, and scalability in NBS projects.

• For example, blockchain can ensure transparency in funding, while AI models optimize intervention designs.

b. Expansion of Open-Source Tools

• Developing open-source digital platforms democratizes access to technology, enabling smaller organizations and communities to participate in NBS initiatives.

c. Policy Advocacy

• Collaborative partnerships can influence policy by demonstrating the effectiveness of technology-enabled NBS, advocating for supportive regulations and funding.

Chapter 10: Challenges and Future Prospects in Digitalizing Nature-Based Solutions

The integration of digital technologies into NBS offers transformative potential for addressing climate change, biodiversity loss, and sustainability challenges. However, the journey toward digitalizing NBS is not without obstacles. Issues such as data accessibility, technological costs, digital literacy, and ethical considerations present significant challenges. At the same time, emerging trends in technology and innovation offer exciting opportunities to enhance the effectiveness and scalability of NBS.

This chapter explores the key challenges facing the digitalization of NBS, including barriers to implementation, the risk of over-reliance on technology, and the need for inclusive and ethical frameworks. It also highlights future prospects, such as advancements in AI, IoT, and blockchain, as well as the role of international collaboration and policy support. By addressing these challenges and leveraging emerging opportunities, stakeholders can ensure that digitalization drives impactful, equitable, and sustainable solutions.

Addressing Barriers Such as Funding, Digital Literacy, and Access to Technology in Digitalizing NBS

The integration of digital technologies into NBS offers significant potential to address environmental challenges, yet various barriers hinder its widespread adoption. Funding constraints, gaps in digital literacy, and limited access to technology are among the most pressing obstacles. Addressing these barriers is essential to ensure that the benefits of digitalizing NBS can be realized equitably and effectively across diverse contexts and regions. This section explores these challenges and provides strategies to overcome them, enabling inclusive and scalable implementation of NBS projects.

1. Overcoming Funding Constraints

a. The Challenge

Digitalizing NBS often requires significant financial investment in technology, infrastructure, training, and ongoing maintenance. For many organizations, particularly those operating in resource-constrained regions, securing sufficient funding is a major challenge:

• **High Initial Costs:** Purchasing and deploying technologies such as IoT sensors, drones, or advanced analytics platforms can strain budgets.

• **Ongoing Operational Costs:** Maintaining digital systems, including cloud subscriptions, data storage, and technical support, adds to financial burdens.

• **Limited Funding Sources:** Environmental organizations often rely on grants and donations, which may not prioritize digital innovation.

b. Strategies for Addressing Funding Challenges

• **Public-Private Partnerships (PPPs):** Collaboration between governments, technology providers, and environmental organizations can pool resources and share costs. For example, a tech company might provide in-kind contributions such as software licenses, while governments cover infrastructure investments.

• **CSR:** Engaging private sector companies through CSR programs can generate funding and support for digital NBS initiatives. Companies benefit from the positive environmental impact associated with their brand.

• **Blended Financing Models:** Combining public grants, private investments, and philanthropic donations creates diversified funding streams. For instance, philanthropic foundations might fund pilot projects, while governments and private investors support scaling efforts.

• **Access to Green Financing:** Leveraging green bonds or climate funds, such as the Green Climate Fund (GCF), provides targeted financial support for sustainable and innovative projects.

• **Cost-Effective Solutions:** Open-source software and affordable hardware options reduce the financial barriers for smaller organizations and communities.

2. Bridging the Digital Literacy Gap

a. The Challenge

Digital tools for NBS require a level of technological proficiency that may not be widespread among key stakeholders, including local communities, small organizations, and certain government agencies. Key issues include:

• **Lack of Training:** Stakeholders may lack the knowledge or experience needed to use technologies like GIS, IoT devices, or mobile apps effectively.

• **Generational and Educational Disparities:** Older generations or individuals with limited formal education may face greater difficulties in adopting digital tools.

• **Complex User Interfaces:** Many digital platforms are not designed with non-technical users in mind, further widening the digital literacy gap.

b. Strategies for Enhancing Digital Literacy

• **Training Programs and Workshops:** Organize hands-on training sessions tailored to the needs of different stakeholder groups. For example, workshops on using GIS for mapping ecosystems or apps for biodiversity monitoring can build confidence and skills.

• **Localized Capacity Building:** Partner with local institutions, such as schools or community centers, to provide ongoing support and mentorship for digital literacy initiatives.

• **Simplified and Inclusive Interfaces:** Design user-friendly platforms that cater to varying levels of expertise. Features such as intuitive navigation, multilingual support, and visual aids make tools more accessible.

• **Digital Ambassadors:** Establish local digital ambassadors who can provide peer-to-peer training and act as liaisons between communities and project managers.

• **Educational Resources:** Create videos, guides, and tutorials that explain digital tools in simple terms, ensuring that materials are culturally and linguistically relevant.

3. Expanding Access to Technology

a. The Challenge

Many communities and organizations, particularly in rural or underserved regions, lack access to the technology needed to participate in digitalized NBS projects. Barriers include:

• **Lack of Devices:** Smartphones, tablets, IoT sensors, and other necessary tools may be unavailable or unaffordable.

• **Poor Connectivity:** Limited access to reliable internet or electricity hampers the use of cloud-based platforms and real-time monitoring technologies.

• **Infrastructure Gaps:** Remote areas often lack the infrastructure to support the deployment of advanced technologies.

b. Strategies for Improving Technology Access

• **Affordable Technology Solutions:** Partner with technology providers to offer subsidized or donated devices, such as smartphones, tablets, or sensors, to organizations and communities in need.

• **Community Technology Hubs:** Establish shared digital hubs equipped with computers, internet access, and charging facilities in local schools or community centers.

• **Offline Functionality:** Design digital tools that work offline or require minimal connectivity, ensuring that data collection and analysis can continue even in remote areas.

• **Decentralized Energy Solutions:** Deploy renewable energy solutions, such as solar-powered charging stations, to support the use of technology in areas with unreliable electricity.

• **Mobile Connectivity Initiatives:** Collaborate with telecommunications companies to expand internet coverage in rural areas, ensuring that remote stakeholders can access cloud-based platforms and digital tools.

• **Low-Tech Alternatives:** Where advanced technology is impractical, provide simpler, low-cost tools that still enable participation. For example, distribute basic data collection kits that can later be digitized.

4. Integrating Inclusive Approaches

a. Ensuring Equity in Digitalization

Efforts to overcome funding, literacy, and access barriers must prioritize inclusivity to ensure that no groups are left behind:

• **Focus on Marginalized Communities:** Tailor interventions to the needs of groups most at risk of exclusion, including women, indigenous peoples, and individuals with disabilities.

• **Participatory Design:** Engage local communities in the design and deployment of digital tools to ensure that solutions align with their needs and capacities.

• **Cultural Sensitivity:** Adapt technologies and training materials to reflect the cultural and linguistic contexts of target communities.

b. The Role of Policy and Advocacy

Policymakers and advocacy groups play a critical role in creating an enabling environment for digitalizing NBS:

• **Incentivizing Innovation:** Governments can provide tax incentives or grants to encourage private sector investment in digital NBS tools.

• **Regulatory Support:** Clear regulations on data privacy, ownership, and usage foster trust in digital platforms.

• **Global Cooperation:** International organizations can facilitate knowledge sharing, capacity building, and funding for digitalization efforts in low-resource settings.

Potential Risks of Over-Reliance on Technology and Maintaining the Balance with Nature

As digital technologies become increasingly integrated into NBS, they bring undeniable benefits for scaling, monitoring, and optimizing these interventions. However, over-reliance on technology poses risks that could undermine the effectiveness, equity, and sustainability of NBS. These risks include the marginalization of traditional ecological knowledge, the detachment of communities from nature, and the vulnerability of technology-dependent systems. Balancing the use of digital tools with the intrinsic principles of NBS is essential to maintain harmony between innovation and natural systems. This section explores the potential risks of over-reliance on technology and outlines strategies to ensure a balanced approach.

1. Risks of Over-Reliance on Technology

a. Marginalization of Traditional Ecological Knowledge

One of the greatest strengths of NBS lies in the integration of traditional and local ecological knowledge, which has been cultivated over generations. Over-reliance on technology can overshadow or exclude this knowledge:

• **Data-Driven Decisions:** While digital tools rely on quantitative data, traditional knowledge often provides qualitative insights that are equally valuable. Focusing solely on data risks neglecting critical context-specific wisdom.

• **Loss of Local Agency:** Communities that have historically managed ecosystems may feel disempowered if decision-making shifts to external experts using advanced technologies.

For example, a reforestation project might prioritize carbon sequestration metrics derived from AI models while overlooking indigenous practices that promote biodiversity and ecosystem resilience.

b. Detachment from Nature

Excessive reliance on technology risks creating a disconnect between people and nature, particularly in urban settings:

• **Virtual Engagement Over Physical Interaction:** Digital tools such as VR and remote monitoring can reduce the need for direct engagement with ecosystems, potentially diminishing people's appreciation of natural systems.

• **Loss of Environmental Stewardship:** When technologies automate tasks like monitoring or maintenance, communities may feel less responsible for the ecosystems around them.

c. Vulnerability to System Failures

Technology-dependent NBS projects are inherently vulnerable to system failures and external threats:

• **Cybersecurity Risks:** Data breaches, hacking, or unauthorized access to digital platforms can compromise sensitive environmental and community data.

• **System Malfunctions:** Failures in IoT sensors, drones, or software platforms can disrupt real-time monitoring and decision-making processes.

• **Dependence on Connectivity:** Remote areas with unreliable internet or electricity face challenges in maintaining the functionality of digital systems.

d. High Costs and Inequities

The cost of acquiring, maintaining, and updating digital technologies can create inequities in NBS implementation:

• Wealthier regions may adopt advanced tools, while resource-constrained areas struggle to participate.

• Communities lacking access to digital infrastructure may be excluded from decision-making processes, exacerbating existing inequalities.

2. Maintaining the Balance with Nature

To address the risks of over-reliance on technology, it is essential to adopt strategies that integrate innovation with the principles of ecological harmony and community involvement.

a. Prioritizing Nature-Centric Approaches

While technology can enhance NBS, the natural systems themselves must remain central to any intervention:

• **Nature First:** Design interventions that prioritize the restoration and preservation of ecosystems, with technology serving as a supportive tool rather than the primary focus.

• **Biodiversity as a Metric:** Ensure that technological innovations promote biodiversity and ecosystem health, rather than focusing solely on metrics like carbon sequestration or cost efficiency.

For example, rewilding projects can use digital tools to monitor species reintroduction, but the primary goal should remain restoring natural processes.

b. Integrating Traditional Knowledge with Technology

Combining traditional ecological knowledge with digital tools creates holistic solutions that respect local contexts:

• **Co-Creation:** Involve indigenous and local communities in the design and implementation of NBS, ensuring their knowledge informs technological applications.

• **Knowledge Sharing Platforms:** Develop platforms that incorporate both traditional practices and modern data, allowing stakeholders to learn from multiple perspectives.

For instance, a watershed management project might integrate local knowledge of seasonal water flows with IoT sensor data to optimize water distribution.

c. Encouraging Hands-On Community Engagement

Maintaining a connection to nature is critical for fostering environmental stewardship:

• **Physical Participation:** Encourage communities to engage directly in activities such as tree planting, habitat restoration, and wildlife monitoring, complementing digital tools with hands-on involvement.

• **Education and Awareness:** Use technology to educate communities about the importance of ecosystems, while providing opportunities for direct interaction with nature.

For example, an urban park project might use AR to teach visitors about local biodiversity while encouraging them to participate in maintenance activities.

3. Building Resilient and Inclusive Systems

Ensuring that technology serves as a reliable and equitable enabler of NBS requires proactive measures to address vulnerabilities and inequalities.

a. Mitigating Vulnerabilities

• **Redundancy and Backup Systems:** Establish backup systems to ensure continuity in monitoring and management during technology failures.

• **Cybersecurity Measures:** Implement robust data protection protocols to safeguard sensitive information from breaches or misuse.

• **Offline Functionality:** Design tools that can operate offline or with minimal connectivity to ensure resilience in remote or resource-constrained areas.

For instance, a reforestation monitoring app could allow users to log data offline, syncing with cloud systems when connectivity is available.

b. Promoting Equity

• **Affordable Solutions:** Advocate for open-source platforms and affordable hardware to reduce financial barriers for under-resourced regions.

• **Capacity Building:** Invest in training programs to equip communities and local organizations with the skills needed to use digital tools effectively.

• **Inclusive Decision-Making:** Ensure that all stakeholders, particularly marginalized groups, have a voice in NBS governance, regardless of their access to technology.

4. Future Opportunities for Balance

The evolving landscape of digital innovation presents opportunities to maintain a balanced approach to NBS while addressing risks.

a. Nature-Inspired Technologies

Advances in biomimicry and nature-inspired designs can align technological innovations more closely with ecological principles:

• For example, drones inspired by the flight patterns of bees can support pollination efforts in degraded ecosystems.

b. Hybrid Systems

Adopting hybrid approaches that combine traditional practices with technology can ensure sustainability and inclusivity:

• For instance, agroforestry projects might use AI to analyze soil health while relying on indigenous planting techniques.

c. Policy and Advocacy

Policymakers play a critical role in guiding the responsible use of technology in NBS:

• Establish guidelines that prioritize ecological integrity and community well-being.

• Advocate for international collaboration to share best practices and resources.

Emerging Trends in the Digitalization of Nature-Based Solutions and Areas for Future Research

The digitalization of NBS is rapidly evolving, driven by technological advancements and increasing recognition of the need for scalable, effective solutions to global environmental challenges. Emerging trends in digital tools, data management, and stakeholder engagement are shaping the future of NBS, offering opportunities to optimize their design, implementation, and impact. However, these advancements also raise important questions and knowledge gaps that require further research to fully realize their potential. This section explores the latest trends in the digitalization of NBS and identifies key areas for future investigation.

1. Emerging Trends in the Digitalization of NBS

a. Integration of Artificial Intelligence and Machine Learning

AI and ML are becoming central to the digitalization of NBS, enabling sophisticated data analysis, predictive modeling, and decision support:

• **Predictive Ecosystem Modeling:** AI-powered tools analyze large datasets to predict the outcomes of NBS interventions, such as carbon sequestration, flood mitigation, or biodiversity recovery. For example, ML algorithms can model how reforestation projects will influence regional climate patterns.

• **Risk Assessment:** AI enhances the identification and management of risks, such as pest outbreaks, soil erosion, or invasive species. By analyzing historical and real-time data, stakeholders can implement proactive measures.

• **Automated Monitoring:** AI-driven image recognition tools are increasingly used to identify species, track changes in vegetation, or detect pollution levels in ecosystems.

b. Expanded Use of Internet of Things

IoT devices are revolutionizing real-time monitoring and adaptive management of NBS:

• **Sensor Networks:** IoT sensors measure parameters such as soil moisture, air quality, water levels, and temperature, providing continuous data streams for ecosystem management.

• **Smart Cities Integration:** Urban NBS, such as green roofs or parks, are being integrated into smart city frameworks, with IoT devices tracking their environmental and social benefits.

• **Low-Power Devices:** Advances in IoT technology are making devices more energy-efficient and affordable, enabling wider deployment in remote or resource-constrained areas.

c. Digital Twin Technology

Digital twins are virtual replicas of ecosystems or landscapes that simulate and test NBS interventions before implementation:

• **Scenario Testing:** Digital twins allow stakeholders to explore various scenarios, such as the impact of different planting densities in reforestation projects or the effectiveness of wetlands in flood mitigation.

• **Ecosystem Visualization:** By creating dynamic, interactive models, digital twins improve stakeholder understanding and engagement, fostering support for NBS initiatives.

• **Integration with Real-Time Data:** Linking digital twins to IoT sensors ensures that models remain accurate and up-to-date, supporting adaptive management.

d. Blockchain for Transparency and Trust

Blockchain technology is emerging as a powerful tool for enhancing transparency, accountability, and collaboration in NBS:

• **Carbon Credit Verification:** Blockchain ensures the integrity of carbon offset projects by providing an immutable record of emissions reductions achieved through NBS.

• **Funding and Governance:** Blockchain-based platforms facilitate transparent allocation and tracking of resources in large-scale NBS projects.

• **Decentralized Collaboration:** By enabling peer-to-peer transactions, blockchain fosters equitable participation among stakeholders, including local communities.

e. Community Engagement Through AR and VR

AR and VR technologies are enhancing community engagement and education in NBS:

• **Interactive Education:** AR apps provide real-time information about local ecosystems, helping communities understand the benefits of NBS.

• **Immersive Experiences:** VR allows stakeholders to explore restored ecosystems or visualize the impacts of degradation, fostering a deeper connection to nature.

• **Participatory Design:** AR tools enable communities to contribute to the planning of NBS, such as designing urban parks or mapping flood-prone areas.

2. Areas for Future Research

While these trends demonstrate significant progress, there are critical knowledge gaps and challenges that require further investigation to optimize the digitalization of NBS.

a. Ethical and Social Implications

The integration of digital technologies into NBS raises important ethical and social questions:

• **Data Privacy:** Research is needed to develop robust frameworks for protecting sensitive environmental and community data collected through IoT sensors or crowdsourcing platforms.

• **Equity in Access:** Future studies should explore strategies to ensure that marginalized communities have equitable access to digital tools and the benefits of NBS.

• **Balancing Technology and Nature:** Investigating the long-term impacts of digitalization on community connections to nature will be critical to maintaining the ecological integrity of NBS.

b. Scalability and Cost-Effectiveness

Scaling up digitalized NBS requires solutions that are cost-effective and adaptable to diverse contexts:

• **Affordable Technologies:** Research should focus on developing low-cost sensors, open-source platforms, and simplified tools for use in resource-constrained regions.

• **Replication Models:** Identifying best practices for replicating successful NBS projects across different landscapes and cultures will enhance scalability.

c. Integration of Traditional Knowledge

The role of traditional ecological knowledge in the digitalization of NBS remains underexplored:

• **Knowledge Co-Creation:** Studies should investigate how to integrate traditional practices with digital tools to create hybrid solutions that respect and leverage local expertise.

• **Community-Led Innovation:** Research on community-driven approaches to digital tool development can ensure that solutions are contextually relevant and culturally appropriate.

d. Interoperability and Data Integration

The success of digitalized NBS depends on seamless data integration across platforms and stakeholders:

• **Standardized Protocols:** Developing standards for data collection, sharing, and analysis will enable better collaboration among governments, NGOs, and private entities.

• **Cross-Sector Applications:** Research should explore how data from NBS projects can inform broader sustainability efforts, such as urban planning or agricultural development.

e. Long-Term Monitoring and Impact Assessment

Assessing the long-term impacts of digitalized NBS remains a critical area for future research:

• **Ecosystem Resilience:** Studies should investigate how digital tools can track the resilience of ecosystems under changing climatic conditions.

• **Socioeconomic Benefits:** Researching the social and economic impacts of NBS, such as improved livelihoods or health outcomes, will strengthen the case for investment.

Conclusion

As we reach the end of this exploration into the digitalization of NBS, it is evident that technology has the power to revolutionize how we address global environmental challenges. From enhancing scalability to improving monitoring and fostering collaboration, digital tools provide unprecedented opportunities to optimize NBS. However, the journey is not without challenges. Balancing the integration of technology with ecological principles and ensuring inclusivity, equity, and ethical considerations are crucial for long-term success.

This concluding chapter synthesizes the key insights from the book, emphasizing the transformative role of digital technologies while underscoring the need for caution and balance. It highlights actionable strategies for embracing innovation without compromising the natural essence of NBS. Finally, it offers a forward-looking vision for a future where digital tools and nature work in harmony to build resilient ecosystems and sustainable communities.

Recap of the Role of Digitalization in Advancing NBS for Climate Resilience and Sustainability

NBS are vital for addressing the intertwined challenges of climate change, biodiversity loss, and sustainability. They provide cost-effective and holistic approaches to enhancing climate resilience while delivering multiple ecological, social, and economic benefits. Digitalization has emerged as a transformative force in advancing NBS, enabling their implementation, monitoring, and scaling in ways previously unattainable.

1. Enhancing Implementation Efficiency

Digital tools and technologies streamline the implementation of NBS by providing data-driven insights and precision. GIS and remote sensing allow stakeholders to map ecosystems, identify priority areas, and design interventions tailored to specific environmental conditions. For example, GIS enables detailed analysis of flood-prone zones to guide wetland restoration projects that mitigate flooding. IoT devices further enhance this efficiency by monitoring environmental conditions in real time, ensuring interventions are adaptive and contextually relevant.

Digital platforms also facilitate collaborative governance, bringing together diverse stakeholders to co-create solutions. These platforms allow governments, NGOs, communities, and private sector actors to contribute expertise and resources, ensuring that NBS projects align with local needs and priorities.

2. Optimizing Monitoring and Maintenance

One of the most significant contributions of digitalization is in the monitoring and maintenance of NBS. Technologies such as IoT sensors, drones, and satellite imagery provide real-time data on ecosystem health, enabling continuous oversight. These tools help track metrics such as water quality, air pollution, biodiversity levels, and soil health, offering insights that guide adaptive management strategies.

AI and ML further enhance monitoring capabilities by analyzing vast datasets to detect trends, predict changes, and identify potential risks. For instance, AI can predict the spread of invasive species in a reforestation project, allowing stakeholders to implement timely control measures.

Digital twins—virtual replicas of ecosystems—have also revolutionized monitoring. These tools simulate various scenarios, allowing stakeholders to test interventions and assess their impacts before implementation. By visualizing ecosystem dynamics, digital twins provide a deeper understanding of how NBS interact with natural and human systems over time.

3. Scaling Up for Greater Impact

Digitalization has made it possible to scale up NBS projects to regional, national, and global levels. Cloud computing and big data analytics provide the computational power needed to manage large-scale interventions. By integrating diverse datasets, stakeholders can replicate successful projects across different contexts, maximizing their impact.

Blockchain technology enhances scalability by fostering transparency and trust in NBS governance. It ensures accountability in funding, carbon credit verification, and resource allocation, making large-scale projects more efficient and equitable.

4. Promoting Community Engagement and Inclusivity

Digital tools have transformed community engagement in NBS, making participation more accessible and impactful. Mobile apps, AR, and VR enable communities to contribute data, learn about ecosystem benefits, and participate in decision-making processes. Crowdsourcing platforms and citizen science initiatives empower individuals to co-create solutions, fostering a sense of ownership and responsibility for local ecosystems.

By integrating traditional ecological knowledge with digital tools, stakeholders ensure that NBS remain culturally relevant and inclusive. This combination of modern technology and traditional wisdom strengthens the effectiveness and sustainability of interventions.

The digitalization of NBS has unlocked new possibilities for addressing climate resilience and sustainability. By enhancing implementation, monitoring, scaling, and community engagement, digital tools ensure that NBS deliver tangible benefits for ecosystems and societies. However, as we embrace these innovations, it is crucial to maintain a balance with nature, ensuring that digitalization complements rather than overshadows the core principles of NBS. This harmonious integration of technology and nature will be key to building a resilient and sustainable future.

Call to Action for Embracing Innovative Technologies While Maintaining Ecological Integrity

The digitalization of NBS presents a transformative opportunity to address the pressing challenges of climate change, biodiversity loss, and sustainable development. Technologies such as AI, IoT, blockchain, and digital twin systems have the potential to optimize NBS implementation, monitoring, and scalability. However, as we integrate these innovative tools into environmental solutions, it is vital to ensure that ecological integrity remains at the forefront of all efforts.

1. Prioritize Nature as the Core Focus

Technology should serve as a tool to enhance NBS, not as a replacement for the fundamental principles of working with nature. As stakeholders embrace digital innovations, they must ensure that:

• **Ecosystems are Restored and Preserved:** The primary goal of NBS must remain the restoration and preservation of ecosystems, with technology acting as a support mechanism rather than a driver.

• **Biodiversity is Fostered:** Technological interventions should enhance, not compromise, biodiversity. Solutions must prioritize species diversity, ecosystem health, and the provision of ecosystem services.

For example, AI-driven models that optimize reforestation efforts must account for diverse plant species and ecological balance rather than solely focusing on carbon sequestration.

2. Promote Inclusive and Ethical Digitalization

For NBS to be truly sustainable, the integration of digital technologies must be inclusive and equitable. This means ensuring that:

• **Communities are Engaged:** Local communities should be active participants in NBS projects, using digital tools to contribute data, provide feedback, and co-create solutions. Citizen science platforms and mobile apps can empower individuals to take ownership of their environments.

• **Traditional Knowledge is Respected:** Indigenous and local ecological knowledge must be integrated with technological insights to create holistic solutions that are culturally and contextually relevant.

• **Access Barriers are Addressed:** Digital tools must be designed to accommodate resource-constrained regions, with affordable, user-friendly, and offline-compatible solutions to bridge the digital divide.

Ethical frameworks must guide the use of data collected through digital tools, ensuring privacy, transparency, and informed consent at every stage.

3. Balance Innovation with Ecological Sensitivity

Over-reliance on technology can create a disconnect from nature and potentially harm the ecosystems it aims to protect. To maintain ecological sensitivity:

• **Limit Automation Where Necessary:** While automation enhances efficiency, physical community engagement in activities such as tree planting and ecosystem monitoring is essential for fostering environmental stewardship.

• **Adopt Hybrid Approaches:** Combining digital tools with traditional practices ensures that solutions are both innovative and grounded in natural principles.

• **Continuously Monitor Impact:** Regularly evaluate the ecological impacts of digital interventions to ensure they align with long-term sustainability goals.

4. Foster Collaboration for Scalable Solutions

Scaling up NBS through digital tools requires collaboration across sectors and regions. Governments, technology providers, NGOs, and communities must work together to:

• **Share Knowledge and Resources:** Open-source platforms and cross-sector partnerships can democratize access to digital tools and expertise.

• **Advocate for Supportive Policies:** Governments should create regulatory frameworks and incentives that encourage the ethical and inclusive use of technology in NBS.

The integration of innovative technologies into NBS is a pivotal step toward addressing global environmental challenges. However, this digital transformation must be pursued with care, ensuring that ecological integrity remains central to all efforts. By prioritizing nature, promoting inclusivity, balancing innovation with sensitivity, and fostering collaboration, stakeholders can harness the power of technology to create resilient, sustainable solutions for the future. Let us embrace these tools as enablers, not substitutes, for the natural systems upon which all life depends.

Vision for a Future Where Technology and Nature Work in Harmony

The future of sustainable development lies at the intersection of technology and nature. As we face unprecedented environmental challenges—ranging from climate change to biodiversity loss and ecosystem degradation—it has become clear that innovative solutions are required. However, these solutions must not replace or overshadow the vital role of natural systems. Instead, the vision for the future is one where technology complements and enhances the inherent capabilities of nature, creating a synergistic relationship that fosters resilience, equity, and sustainability.

1. A World Driven by Ecological Wisdom and Technological Innovation

The harmonious integration of technology and nature starts with recognizing that ecosystems possess unique, irreplaceable qualities. Nature's resilience, self-regulating mechanisms, and ability to provide ecosystem services form the foundation of this vision. In this future:

• **Technology Acts as an Enabler:** Digital tools such as AI, IoT sensors, and blockchain technology support the protection, restoration, and monitoring of ecosystems without disrupting their natural processes.

• **Nature Remains Central:** NBS projects, such as reforestation, wetland restoration, and urban greening, are driven by the principles of ecological integrity, with technology serving to amplify their effectiveness.

For instance, IoT sensors might monitor soil health in a reforested area, providing data to guide adaptive management while allowing the forest to evolve naturally over time.

2. Inclusive and Collaborative Solutions

The future envisions an inclusive framework where communities, policymakers, scientists, and technologists collaborate to co-create solutions that respect both local contexts and global challenges. In this ideal scenario:

• **Communities are Empowered:** Digital tools democratize participation in environmental decision-making, enabling individuals to contribute data, provide feedback, and play an active role in safeguarding ecosystems.

• **Traditional Knowledge Meets Innovation:** Indigenous ecological knowledge is integrated into digital platforms, enriching data-driven solutions with centuries of wisdom.

• **Accessible Technologies for All:** Affordable, user-friendly digital tools bridge the gap between resource-rich and resource-constrained regions, ensuring that the benefits of technology and NBS reach everyone.

For example, a coastal community using AR to visualize rising sea levels and plan mangrove restoration also integrates local knowledge of tidal patterns to enhance project outcomes.

3. Dynamic and Resilient Ecosystems

In this vision, ecosystems thrive under the dual stewardship of natural processes and technological advancements. Real-time data and predictive modeling ensure that interventions adapt to changing conditions, fostering long-term resilience. Key elements include:

• **Digital Twins for Ecosystem Simulation:** Virtual replicas of ecosystems provide stakeholders with insights into potential outcomes of various interventions, enabling informed, proactive decision-making.

• **Nature-Inspired Technologies:** Biomimicry drives innovation, with technologies mimicking natural processes to enhance efficiency and sustainability. For instance, AI algorithms inspired by the behavior of bees optimize pollination strategies.

This dynamic approach ensures that ecosystems are protected and enhanced, even in the face of climate uncertainty.

4. A Culture of Stewardship and Sustainability

The harmonious future is not only about technological and ecological integration but also about fostering a cultural shift. Individuals, organizations, and governments embrace environmental stewardship as a shared responsibility:

• **Technology Enhances Awareness:** VR and educational apps immerse people in the beauty and complexity of ecosystems, fostering a deeper connection to nature.

• **Sustainable Practices Become Norms:** Data-driven insights guide sustainable behaviors in agriculture, urban planning, and energy use, creating a world where human activity aligns with ecological health.

For instance, urban planners design green spaces using predictive analytics, ensuring that cities serve as habitats for both people and wildlife.

5. A Global Network of Innovation and Cooperation

In this vision, nations and organizations collaborate across borders to share knowledge, resources, and technologies:

• **Open-Source Platforms:** Tools and data are freely shared, enabling global participation in tackling environmental challenges.

• **Policy Alignment:** Governments harmonize regulations to support the ethical use of technology in NBS, ensuring accountability and inclusivity.

The result is a globally connected effort to address climate change, conserve biodiversity, and build sustainable communities.

The future where technology and nature work in harmony is one of hope, innovation, and resilience. It envisions a world where natural systems thrive alongside technological advancements, each enhancing the other's strengths. By prioritizing ecological integrity, fostering inclusivity, and embracing collaboration, we can build a sustainable and equitable future. This vision inspires action, reminding us that the best solutions are those where humanity acts as a steward, not a disruptor, of the natural world.

.

www.ingramcontent.com/pod-product-compliance
Lightning Source LLC
Chambersburg PA
CBHW052129270326
41930CB00012B/2818